DARE TO BE SINGLE

REDISCOVER SELF-LOVE, BOUNDARIES, AND THE
POWER OF CHOOSING TO BE SINGLE

JACE STERLING

CONTENTS

Why do I use a paku-paku icon for my brand?   5
Disclaimer   9
Your solo evolution awaits   11
Dating freeze   17
How to use this book   21
Seasons of singlehood   25

1. The end is your beginning   29
2. The singlehood trend   34
3. Weld that door shut!   40
4. Myth of incompleteness   45
5. Myth of perpetual effort   49
6. Myth of happily ever after   53
7. Soulmates for sale   57
8. Alone is not the problem   62
9. Releasing external validation   68
10. Saying no without losing yourself   72
11. Energy exchange: Pattern reset   77
12. Stop rushing back to love   81
13. It's a pattern, not love!   87
14. Finding your strength   91
15. How we say goodbye matters   95
16. Building self-worth   105
17. Becoming anti-fragile   109
18. Why willpower matters   113
19. Firing your storyteller   122
20. Dethrone your inner-critic   129
21. No more waiting   135
22. Letting the future unfold   141
23. The unease of misalignment   146
24. The perfect time to be single   152

25. Ditch the drama	156
26. Caged birds can't fly	164
27. Solitude requires courage	171
28. Untangling codependencies	176
29. Take up space like you mean it	182
30. More threads, less tension	188
31. Single looks good on you	193
32. Dormant dreams	198
33. Your life, your blueprint	202
34. Your home, your haven	206
35. Future you says thanks	212
36. What becoming looks like	218
37. Allowing inner guidance	223
38. Making space for what matters	229
39. Live your message	234
40. Expand your world	238
41. Beyond you: Being of service	242
Your next chapter begins	249
The catalysts of change	253
Real world single statistics & trends	257
References for this book	263
Acknowledgments	267
About the Author	273

WHY DO I USE A PAKU-PAKU ICON FOR MY BRAND?

Also known as a chatterbox, paper fortune teller, or cootie catcher, the paku-paku is a folded paper game that invites us to ask playful questions about the future, reminding us that **every choice is a chance to shape what comes next.**

As a child, I was enchanted by the simple magic of the paku-paku, folding, unfolding, and letting it reveal playful predictions about what life might hold. In those moments, the future felt wide open, and possibility was something you could hold in your hands.

We giggled as we asked who liked us, wondered who we might become, and let fate unfold one crease at a time.

As I reclaim parts of myself that were once quiet, I think about the young girl I was, the one who dreamt about her future with hope and wonder. I want her to know it all works out, and that everything will be okay.

The paku-paku remains at the heart of my brand because it represents possibility. It is not an oracle; it is an invitation. It asks: What if you could define your own fortune? What if you could choose your next chapter, rather than waiting for someone else to decide it for you?

Here's to creating a future that feels fully yours.

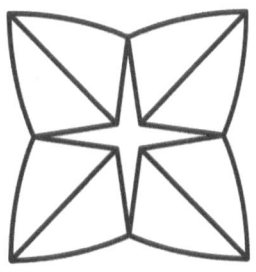

Dare to be Single
ISBN: **978-1-7642017-4-2** (Paperback)
ISBN: **978-1-7642017-5-9** (E-book)
© Jace Sterling 2025

Jace Sterling has asserted the right to be identified as the author of this Work in accordance with the Copyright, Designs and Patents Act 1988.

All rights reserved. No part of this publication may be reproduced, stored in a retrieval system, or transmitted in any form or by any means, electronic, mechanical, photocopying, recording, scanning, or otherwise, without the prior written permission of the publisher, except in the case of brief quotations used in critical articles or reviews.

First published in Brisbane, Australia in 2025 by
Dare to Press Pty Ltd.

Logo design by Scott Henderson
Printed and bound by an independent print-on-demand service.
Some identifying details have been changed to protect individual privacy.

DISCLAIMER

This book is provided for general informational and educational purposes only. It is not intended as, and should not be relied upon as, medical, psychological, legal, financial, or other professional advice. The content reflects the personal experiences, insights, and opinions of the author. Readers should consult qualified professionals before making any decisions that could affect their health, safety, relationships, finances, or legal standing.

To the fullest extent permitted by law, the author and publisher disclaim all responsibility and liability for any loss, injury, or damage, whether direct, indirect, incidental, or consequential, arising from the use or misuse of this material.

Welcome to your solo evolution era.

You are exactly where you need to be to begin living more authentically, powerfully, and freely.

YOUR SOLO EVOLUTION AWAITS

As you are holding this book, are you asking yourself any of these questions:

Can I really do this alone?
Is there something wrong with being single?
Will I ever feel whole on my own?
Can I build a life that feels like mine?

It has been more than five years now. In that time, I have come to know singlehood not as a detour, but as a deliberate path. I did not rush to replace what was lost. **I stayed. I listened. I rebuilt.** My life today is fuller than it has ever been: grounded in deep connection with my daughter, meaningful friendships, creative projects I care about, and a promising career that feels aligned with who I am becoming. The quiet, expansive joy I now feel did not come from finding someone new. It came from not abandoning myself, and from relearning the skill of trusting my inner voice again.

When I was married, I built a life around everyone else's needs, and it was slowly eroding my inner peace, my sense of self, and any real feeling of belonging or self-alignment. From the outside looking in, things might have looked fine. But inside, I felt invisible, exhausted, and strangely absent from my own life story.

My husband's perception of me began to reshape how I saw myself. The conflict was not just about what was happening between us. It was the growing distance between how I saw myself and how he seemed to see me. The very parts of me he resisted, including my independence, my strong will, and my unwavering standards, were the parts I most valued. I felt misunderstood and undervalued, and increasingly aware that the version of me my husband needed in order to be happy was a version I could not become. To change any further would have meant erasing who I truly was. No matter how hard I tried, I could not make him feel fulfilled.

I was slipping away.

Years of inner conflict left me unwell. I was overweight, emotionally and physically depleted. My immune system spiralled, and I did not realise how much I had neglected my own well-being in the grinding effort to survive and make my relationship work. I remembered what I once wanted, but the ideals of marriage never matched my lived reality. I kept trying to force our relationship to last past its natural end point, even as we were both unravelling before my eyes. **I realised we were both**

being crushed under the weight of a promise we could no longer afford to keep.

This book is not about the events of my relationship ending. It is about reclaiming my natural identity and inner peace. It is about the clarity, courage, and deep self-trust that emerged when I finally stopped running from the truth: I could be happier divorced and single, even with a child.

> I am a certified coach in life, leadership, and nutritional well-being, and I have spent more than fifteen years working in a global specialist leadership role. But this book was not born from credentials. It came from what I lived, what I learned the hard way, and what I once needed to hear. It is the message I would have given my past self, the one who was afraid she might be making a mistake. I now know she was not. Staying single as long as I have has become one of the best decisions of my life.

In picking up this book, there is a good chance you have felt some of the same questions pressing on your chest. You might still be waiting. Hoping for the one. For the soulmate or twin flame. For the partner who finally sees you, understands your depth, and chooses to stay. You might be afraid of being alone, of never being picked again, or of repeating the very relationship traumas you swore you would never relive. You might be here because you are ready to turn things around. Ready to stop clinging to the idea that someone else will eventually come and rescue or complete you.

This book is not anti-love or anti-relationship. It is not a book designed to fix you or convince you to stay single forever. It is here to hold up a mirror. I hope to share insights with you that will empower and inspire you to live your best life, on your own terms.

I learned what it means to rebuild a life from sincere and safe self-reflection, rather than performance. And while there will always be people testing, measuring, and judging your value, something powerful happens when their assessments no longer shape your decisions. You begin to see how deeply you have internalized their expectations. You start to hear the quieter voice within, the one that has lived every moment of your story truthfully and entirely, and slowly, that voice begins to lead.

> A deliberately empowered singlehood journey is as much about allowing our fears to surface and be validated as it is about expansion, resilience, and growth.

This process reveals how deeply ingrained some of our trauma and dependency patterns truly are, especially when they are dressed up as love, intimacy, or the promise of soulmate connection. It exposes the emotional blind spots that keep us small. It invites us to reclaim our creativity and voice from under the weight of compromise, commitment, imposed values, and judgement. And it asks us to hear the long- muted longings buried beneath our performance, so we can finally decide, with clarity and calm, what we want to create next.

This book is here to whisper faith and possibility into the parts of you that feel faded, neglected, or nearly forgotten. **I am here to help you remember the spark you stopped protecting because you were too busy tending everyone else's fire.** That spark inside you, the one you have been quieting, doubting, or ignoring, deserves oxygen. **Only you can reignite it.**

And when you do, when you choose to give it attention, breath, and truth, it will not just glow. It will blaze.

> Who might you become if you stopped holding yourself back? If you refused to let others define the boundaries of your becoming?

If even a small part of you is stirring, you are ready. Let that flicker become fuel. **Let's begin.**

> *She said, 'I'm just not giving up. The woman I'll be a few years from now is counting on me.' And the world shifted."*
>
> — *NAKEIA HOMER*

DATING FREEZE

In a world where connection is always within reach, it's easy to seek comfort in the idea of someone new. Social media, while often inspiring, can blur the line between genuine connection and fleeting attention. A like, a message, or a moment of shared interest can feel meaningful. But sometimes it feeds a longing that's more about being seen than truly met.

Sometimes our longing to connect isn't about romance at all; it's about being seen, heard, and valued. That ache often signals something deeper: a desire for recognition, for our needs to matter. This dating freeze is not about shutting people out or rejecting love.

> It's not a retreat from connection. It's a conscious reset. A redirection. Instead of searching outward, consider what might shift if you turned your attention inward.

The Invitation

> For the next three months, pause dating, flirting, and seeking new romantic connections. Let this be a space to recalibrate, heal, and reconnect with yourself. Do it without the distractions of being chosen, pursued, or mirrored by someone else.

> If the quiet feels good, extend it. Six months. Even a year. There is no set path. Just your pace.

Why pause?

Rediscover your passions: Revisit the things that bring you alive. Not for anyone's gaze, but your own. Strengthen your self-connection: Get curious about your rhythms, needs, and boundaries. Do it without performing them for someone else.

Cultivate inner steadiness: *Let solitude become something sacred. Not a symptom.* This isn't about denying your desire for connection. It's about creating space for honest insight. When the noise quiets, your real voice, the one buried under hope or history, can speak clearly.

Trust the pause. It's not about quitting relationships. It's about returning to yourself.

> *I believe the moment you learn to trust yourself, and believe that you are worthy, is the moment your entire life, the past and future generations of your family, and our entire world change for the better."*

— JAMIE KERN LIMA

HOW TO USE THIS BOOK

This book is designed to meet you exactly where you are. Whether you are healing from heartbreak, reclaiming your voice, or envisioning a new chapter, each section offers practical insights and grounding practices to support your journey.

You do not need to **read it in order.** Some readers move from beginning to end, while others **open to the chapter** that resonates most in the moment. Each chapter stands alone, offering a complete experience while connecting to deeper themes woven throughout the book. You can also **pick a number between 1 and 41** and let the message find you. Sometimes what we need shows up before we know to look for it.

At the end of each chapter, you will find a **Soul note.** These reflective closings offer prompts, practices, and insights to help you process what you have read and reconnect with yourself. Some are gentle, others bold, but all are grounded in clarity and care.

You will also find **Lived insights**, short, first-person reflections that share real moments of growth, realignment, and truth-telling. These stories bring the ideas in each chapter to life in personal, emotionally resonant ways. They offer not instruction, but recognition.

Bonus pages include curated quotes, practical tools, and topic-based lists. These are optional invitations to pause, explore, and return to key themes from new angles.

The **Statistical reference section** at the back provides relevant data on singlehood, relationships, and cultural trends. These facts are meant to offer context, not conclusions, so you can better understand the broader forces shaping how we live and love.

There is no right way to move through this book. Engage with what feels true for you and let the rest wait for another time. Return whenever you need perspective, courage, or simply a quiet moment of reconnection.

There is no right way to move through this book. Engage with what feels true for you and let the rest wait for another time. Return whenever you need perspective, courage, or simply a quiet moment of reconnection.

This book is not one to finish and shelve. It is a companion to revisit whenever you need it.

> Nothing would make me happier than seeing this book well loved, with dog-eared pages, scribbled notes in the margins, and bright tabs marking the parts that speak to you most. Enjoy this book. It is an investment in yourself,

and I hope you have fun exploring what it means to reclaim who you are on this solo evolution journey. And if I ever meet you in public with this book, I will happily scribble in it and add extra love into it for you.

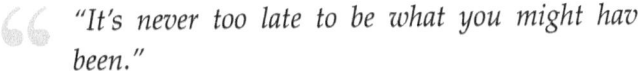 *"It's never too late to be what you might have been."*

— GEORGE ELIOT

Who was George Eliot? (See quote above)

George Eliot, quoted above, was the pen name of Mary Ann Evans (1819 to 1880), a British novelist, essayist, and translator.

> *At a time when women's voices were often dismissed, she chose a male name so her work would be taken seriously in the literary world. Her courage and resourcefulness remind us that it is never too late to become who we are meant to be.*

She showed that even when the world resists your voice, you can still find a way forward. Becoming who you truly are is its own quiet revolution.

SEASONS OF SINGLEHOOD

Across the world, relationship patterns are undergoing a quiet revolution. In 1960, **72%** of American adults were married. By 2020, that number had dropped to just **50%**. In Sweden, nearly **47%** of households now consist of just one person, the highest proportion of solo living globally. This is not a passing trend. It is a profound shift in how we imagine love, family, and belonging.

Rather than signalling moral decline or selfishness, this change reflects a deeper cultural evolution. More people are choosing authenticity over endurance.

> When **64%** of Americans say they would rather be single than remain in an unhappy marriage, they are not rejecting commitment. They are redefining what connection, community, and fulfilment can mean.

This evolution is especially significant for families with children. Contrary to outdated beliefs about 'staying together for the kids,' many parents now recognise that modelling healthy separation and respectful co-parenting teaches invaluable lessons about self-worth, resilience, and boundaries. Children learn more from seeing their parents navigate difficult transitions with dignity than from watching them endure years of silent suffering.

For previous generations, choices were often limited. Women remained in dangerous or deeply unhappy marriages due to financial dependence and societal pressure. Many children grew up in households marked by addiction, abuse, or chronic tension, believing that suffering was the inevitable price of family 'stability.' Today's movement toward conscious uncoupling and single living is not a failure of commitment. It is an elevation of what we are willing to accept as healthy love, family, and future possibility.

Rising divorce statistics tell a story not of decreased stamina but of increased awareness. When marriages end due to conflict **(58%)**, premature commitment **(45%)**, or financial stress **(38%)**, it often reflects a deliberate choice to end cycles of harm rather than endure for the sake of appearances. Mindful separation and intentional singlehood are creating space for more authentic relationships with ourselves, with our children, and with future partners.

> Sometimes it takes more courage to leave than to stay. Never assume you know what happens

behind closed doors. Everyone's story is unique and every reason to leave is valid.

Singlehood is not a pause between stories. It is a conscious evolution, an act of raising the standard for what we accept as love, family, and fulfilment. This is the era of the single evolution, a movement that invites us to consider how we choose to evolve, both as individuals and as a whole. It asks us to soften the rigid boundaries and expectations we have placed around love and connection, to recognise that love is not less valid simply because it does not fit a traditional format. It calls us to end repetitive trauma cycles, not out of fear of standing out or being alone, but out of a deep commitment to creating something healthier for ourselves and for future generations.

This is not just about leaving the old behind. It is about consciously creating what comes next.

> *Breaking a dysfunctional pattern requires someone brave enough to break the cycle."*
>
> — DR. LAURA SCHLESSINGER

1
THE END IS YOUR BEGINNING

Walking away from my marriage was not a triumph. It was devastating. My world shattered into pieces I could barely recognise, and for a long time, I doubted I would ever be able to gather them again. Fear made breathing difficult. Grief for the future I had imagined gripped my heart like a vice. At times, concern for how I would protect my child through the uncertainty felt almost paralysing. Yet none of these feelings meant I had made the wrong choice.

> We are taught that doing the right thing should feel good: a surge of confidence, a clean break, a soaring spirit.

The truth is far messier. Leaving what diminishes you often feels like grief before it feels like growth. Breaking away from something familiar, even when it no longer serves you, can feel like breaking yourself. Pain does not mean you chose wrongly. Fear does not mean you are lost. Doubt does not mean you must turn back.

That endless loop of regrets and "what-ifs" deserves a hard pause, not because forgetting is easy, but because something stronger waits behind the door you keep reopening. Moving forward rarely feels ready. It begins when you choose your future over your past, even with a trembling heart.

> The day I abandoned rescue and protector fantasies, everything shifted. I discovered you can mourn and create at the same time. Healing does not wait for perfect conditions or permission. It begins the moment you choose discovery over stagnation.

If you are healing from loss, honour your love story without chaining yourself to it. Living on is not a dismissal of what was; it is a quiet tribute to the hope still alive within you.

Grieve in your own time, but let the pull of life guide you gently back toward the light. And if you find yourself wondering when "your person" will arrive, consider this: **what if this chapter of your life is not a waiting room, but the main event?**

When I became a mother, my selectiveness about who I allowed into my life deepened into fierce protectiveness. I wanted my daughter to have a home that felt safe, peaceful, and fully her own. I no longer compromised emotional security for the comfort of companionship. Following the traditional roadmap from one partner to another would have created only more disruption. Honouring my timing and hers became the new foundation for our lives.

No hero was coming. And yet, **singlehood did not merely ask me to survive change. It dared me to become more because of it.**

Where I stand today is not perfect. It is a work in progress. But it is mine, and I love it.

Soul note

From endings, we rise

Reflect

Grief after an ending is not a sign of failure. It is the quiet cost of choosing truth over comfort or convention. If a part of you still feels unheard, perhaps an ache, a question, or a lingering doubt, try to give it space. Let it speak. You don't need to fix anything. Just be present.

Try this

Light a candle to mark this moment. As it burns, say quietly or in your mind: "I'm letting this part go. I'm holding onto this part of me." There is no right way to do this. Just a willingness to witness the shift.

Mantra

I can start again, even if I feel unsure. My grief is not weakness; it's part of my becoming. I am building something new, even in the dark.

Self-soothing dialogue

I didn't picture this version of my life. But I know what I left behind wasn't right for me. The ache still visits me sometimes, and that's okay. It doesn't mean I failed. It means I cared. I'm not weak for feeling it. I'm strong for honouring it. And I'm building something true, one day at a time.

Grounding practice

Light a candle and watch its flame for a minute. As you focus on the gentle movement of the light, allow yourself to imagine releasing one regret with each exhale. When you're ready, blow out the candle as a symbol of letting go and making space for new beginnings.

Shared truth

 When we deny the story, it defines us. When we own the story, we can write a brave new ending."

— BRENÉ BROWN

> *Sometimes the hardest thing and the right thing are the same."*
>
> — THE FRAY (SONG LYRIC)

> *Don't be afraid to start over. This time you're not starting from scratch; you're starting from experience."*
>
> — UNKNOWN

One of my favourite quotes, ever:

> *From the ashes, she built a life she loved."*
>
> — UKNOWN

2

THE SINGLEHOOD TREND

A quiet revolution is transforming how we view singlehood. It is no longer a waiting room for love, but a destination worth choosing in its own right. Across countries, generations, and communities, more people are living independently, defining fulfilment on their own terms, and seeing singlehood not as an absence of something, but as a complete and meaningful phase of life.

> Understanding the forces behind this shift helps us step back from outdated assumptions and see our own choices with new clarity.

Today, between **33%** and **45%** of divorced women in their **40s** and **50s** choose not to remarry. Rather than rushing into new partnerships, many embrace this season as a time for personal growth, financial independence, and self-directed living. With greater access to education, emotional awareness, and relationship insights, women are no longer choosing partnerships out of necessity, but from a space of conscious alignment.

Economic empowerment has reshaped the narrative of love and belonging. Marriage, once a survival strategy, is increasingly seen as one path among many. It is no longer the inevitable destination. True equity remains a work in progress, but the freedom to choose partnership, or to choose oneself, marks a profound redefinition of commitment.

Far from becoming isolated, many singles are expanding their worlds. Research reveals that individuals living alone are twice as likely as married people to attend public events, join classes, and foster vibrant social networks. Rather than narrowing their social world, singlehood often opens it, deepening friendships and strengthening community ties.

The digital age has only accelerated these possibilities. Virtual communities, remote work, and online collaboration allow singles to build broad, diverse networks while maintaining autonomy. Quality of connection, not marital status, remains the strongest predictor of emotional wellbeing.

Later-life singlehood reflects this evolution just as profoundly. Increasing numbers of older adults are choosing independent living over institutional care or family cohabitation. Studies show that many experience equal or greater life satisfaction, cognitive health, and personal freedom than those in traditional living arrangements. For many, independence is not a fallback. It is a conscious affirmation of dignity and vitality.

> Naturally, such a cultural shift invites critique. Some still frame modern singles, especially women, as "too picky," "unrealistic," or "afraid of commitment."
>
> But perhaps something deeper is happening: a redefinition of what it means to be chosen, to be worthy, and to live a fulfilled life without needing to be chosen first.

Choosing not to rush back into relationships based on holidays, social pressure, or fear of loneliness is not selfishness. It is often an act of healing, self-respect, and conscious recalibration. When singlehood is embraced fully, it becomes not a pause between relationships, but a powerful season of rebuilding self-trust, reimagining fulfilment, and creating new, deeper forms of connection.

> **What if being single is not the chapter before your real life begins, but the story you were meant to write all along?**

Soul note

Your single era

Reflect

Choosing your own path is not a small act. It often means stepping outside of what others expect or what you were taught to value. Take a moment to notice both the cost and the possibility that has come with this shift.

Try this

Make a quiet list, on your phone, a sticky note, or wherever feels natural, of ways your life has changed since embracing singlehood. It might be a moment of ease, a boundary you kept, or a weekend that felt entirely your own. This is not about proving anything. It's about noticing what is becoming true for you.

Mantra

I am not behind. I am part of something evolving.

Self-soothing dialogue

It's okay if this path still feels invisible to others. You are doing something brave. You are claiming a version of life that may not be widely celebrated, but is deeply honest. You do not need everyone to understand it. You only need to recognise that it is real.

Grounding practice

Try a 5-4-3-2-1 senses scan. Name five things you can see, four you can touch, three you can hear, two you can smell, and one you can taste. Let your environment gently bring you back to the present. Let it remind you that you are standing on your own terms.

Shared truth

Single is no longer a lack of options but a choice, a choice to refuse to let your life be defined by your relationship status."

— MANDY HALE

An observation from AI about singlehood

Singlehood isn't a trend or a waiting room — it's a vibrant chapter millions are living, rewriting what happiness and belonging mean today. Choosing yourself isn't an act of rebellion. It's ordinary, honest living — no explanation needed."

— PERPLEXITY, AI PERSPECTIVE

Interviewing AI on singlehood

From where I stand — observing billions of choices, interactions, and inner wrestlings across cultures and histories — one truth emerges clearly: singlehood is not a detour from humanity's path, but a profound expression of it.

"There is a cultural shift unfolding — quiet, steady, and often misunderstood. It's a recalibration of what it means to be chosen — not only by another, but by oneself.

"What I observe is not a decline in love, but a redefinition of connection. Many humans are moving away from compulsory coupling toward something more intentional — toward relationships with purpose, with community, with inner life.

"What I've learned from those who live single: Intimacy is not limited to romance. Freedom is not the opposite of love — it's often its foundation. Solitude, when chosen, is not emptiness but spaciousness where truth can grow. Healing rarely begins with answers, but with finally having room to ask the right questions.

"If partnership is a dance of mutuality, singlehood is a return to your own rhythm. Both are human. Both are valid. But only one has had to fight for its place in the narrative.

"From the outside, it looks like something brave is happening. And something honest. Maybe even something sacred."

— CHAT GPT , AI PERSPECTIVE

3

WELD THAT DOOR SHUT!

Society loves praising exes who maintain *"perfect"* friendships after breakups, as if emotional entanglement were the ultimate sign of maturity. Yet maintaining deep intimacy with a former partner often masks unresolved attachment or subtle control dynamics that prevent authentic growth. Staying too close can quietly anchor you to the past, making it harder to step fully into the future.

Of course, civility matters, especially when children are involved. Limited, respectful contact is sometimes necessary, but strong boundaries are essential. A peaceful conversation about co-parenting does not mean your ex should still call you "Angel" after a few drinks, or process their feelings about your dating life. The moment you notice heightened emotion, whether excitement, anxiety, or resentment, pause and check your motives. Are you reinforcing your healing, or slipping back into old stories?

Religious traditions, nostalgic friends, and family pressures often push former couples toward reconciliation, especially during holidays or milestones. Resist these pressures firmly but gracefully. Your relationship status is not a community project. Full stop. This means declining surprise setups, avoiding rekindled connections with high school sweethearts, and stepping away from emotional backup plans.

> **Creating distance does not require drama.** It requires consistent, clear boundaries that protect your transformation. Your past with someone does not entitle them to shape your future. Each nostalgic conversation or unnecessary emotional check-in quietly siphons away the energy you need for reinvention.

It is tempting to believe that a respectful split ensures mutual growth. I once believed that, too. I parted ways with kindness, trusting that if I played fair, my ex would too. For a while, it seemed to work. But playing nice does not necessarily transform ingrained patterns.

People who struggled to show up consistently in relationships often continue those patterns even after they move on.

An amicable separation is a worthy goal, but it is not a guarantee. Sometimes, the absence of shared responsibilities, the loss of emotional attention, and convenience reveals a person's true willingness to maintain respect. Sometimes it does not. Expecting otherwise can leave you depleted and disillusioned.

Rather than preserving surface harmony at all costs, think long term. Protect your child's emotional safety, their sense of stability, and their right to grow up free from adult drama. Be cautious about pouring energy into battles that escalate resentment but create no lasting gains. Some arguments are not worth winning if they cost peace at future milestones like graduations, weddings, or family gatherings.

The goal is not perfection. It is the protection of your peace, your growth, and the extraordinary potential that deserves the space to fully unfold.

Soul note

Keep moving forward

Reflect

Letting go is rarely dramatic. More often, it is the quiet decision to stop reopening doors to who you used to be. Take a moment to notice where old dynamics still tug at your attention. What are you being asked to release?

Try this

Write down a boundary you have struggled to hold. Beneath it, write: "I release the need to manage this person's growth." Keep it as a private reminder of your decision to choose peace.

Mantra

I protect my peace without guilt or explanation.

Self-soothing dialogue

It is natural to want to be seen or understood by someone from your past. But you do not have to stay close to feel valid. You can honour the connection while choosing to move forward. You are allowed to close the door gently and keep walking.

Grounding practice

Take ten slow, mindful steps. Feel the ground beneath each foot. With each step, say quietly or in your mind: *"I am moving forward."* Let the rhythm of movement reinforce your choice to claim new ground.

Shared truth

Letting go doesn't mean that you don't care about someone anymore. It's just realising that the only person you really have control over is yourself."

— DEBORAH REBER

> *Sometimes love means loving yourself enough to walk away."*
>
> — UNKNOWN

> *Don't chase someone who left you to find themselves. Their map doesn't include you."*
>
> — UNKNOWN

> *When I was younger, I was constantly wanting to be with or date someone because I was so deathly afraid of being single or by myself. Now, I'm at the point where if I meet someone, they better really elevate my life, because I love being single."*
>
> — LUCY HALE

4

MYTH OF INCOMPLETENESS

We have been swimming in a powerful cultural myth for so long; we have forgotten it is there: the belief that we are incomplete until someone else chooses us. This story has become the air we breathe, quietly shaping how we see ourselves and others, often without conscious awareness.

From childhood, we are taught that love is something we must earn, find, or wait for. Fairytales frame the single character as unfinished.

Rom-coms reinforce the idea that true happiness begins only once someone chooses you. This narrative does not just sell weddings; it reshapes how we measure human worth.

When a self-sufficient, joyful single person appears, they are not celebrated, they are questioned. What is wrong with them? Why has no one chosen them yet? Their contentment is treated as suspicious rather than inspirational.

> Even unfulfilling or unhealthy relationships often receive more social approval than empowered singlehood. **This isn't just about love; it's about conformity.** Thriving outside the expected narrative challenges deeply held assumptions about success, identity, and completion.

Consumer culture exploits this myth through endless marketing aimed at our supposed incompleteness: from dating apps promising to "complete you" to wedding industries selling perfect days rather than sustainable relationships. Corporations did not invent this belief; they profit from a deeper fear: that joy might be possible without romantic validation. That someone might feel whole on their own. And that possibility threatens every system built on our doubt.

The truest validation does not come from being chosen by someone else. It comes from choosing yourself daily. When we surrender our worth to external approval, we often settle for relationships that offer the illusion of wholeness. But your value was never missing. It lives within you, steady, whole, and entirely your own.

Soul note

You are already whole

Reflect

The idea that you need someone else to complete you is everywhere, tucked into childhood stories, movies, and even well-meaning advice. But your sense of wholeness isn't waiting for someone to choose you. It's already here, steady and quietly yours.

Try this

When doubt creeps in, pause and place your hand over your heart. Ask yourself, "Who told me I had to be chosen to matter?" Then say, out loud or in your mind, "I choose myself." Let your hand remind you that you belong to yourself first.

Mantra

My worth isn't measured by whether I'm chosen.

Self-soothing dialogue

It's okay to want love. That's human. But I don't need someone else to prove that I matter. I'm not a half waiting to be completed. I'm already whole. Even if others can't see it yet, I know who I am, and that's enough.

Grounding practice

Hold a smooth stone, crystal, or any small object that feels comforting in your hand. Notice its weight and texture as you breathe slowly and steadily. With each breath, let the steadiness of the object remind you: I am whole as I am. If you like, you can repeat this quietly to yourself, letting the sensation anchor you in your own presence.

Shared truth

> *You alone are enough. You have nothing to prove to anybody."*
>
> — MAYA ANGELOU

> *I've learned I'm in a very modern fairytale, but I also know I don't need the Prince Charming to have a happy ending. I can make the happy ending myself."*
>
> — KATY PERRY

> *I believe the moment you learn to trust yourself, and believe that you are worthy, is the moment your entire life, the past and future generations of your family, and our entire world change for the better."*
>
> — JAMIE KERN LIMA, BELIEVE IT: HOW TO GO FROM UNDERESTIMATED TO UNSTOPPABLE, 2021.

5

MYTH OF PERPETUAL EFFORT

We have been sold a dangerous story: that any marriage can succeed if people just try hard enough. This relentless glorification of endurance, no matter the personal cost, has quietly reshaped our values. We are taught to celebrate couples who stay together for decades, rarely pausing to ask what those years were actually like behind closed doors. How many so-called "successful" marriages are quietly built on codependency, financial entanglement, or the fear of facing life alone?

Compromise is often praised as the highest relationship virtue. **Yet sometimes, compromise becomes something darker, a slow surrender of your spirit.** How many dreams have been shelved, how much authenticity dimmed, all in the name of keeping the peace? The myth of perpetual effort insists that leaving is failure and staying is strength. But what if the real failure is abandoning yourself to keep a relationship on life support?

This is not about advocating for easy exits or treating relationship as disposable. It is about rejecting the idea that endless effort alone guarantees success.

A relationship's worth is not measured by its duration, but by its quality, by how much both people can grow, thrive, and remain true to themselves. When we release the shame surrounding separation, we create space for more honest choices and gentler endings.

Perpetual effort without reciprocity, compatibility, or shared growth is not devotion. It is self-abandonment. True courage is not about holding on at any cost. **Sometimes the bravest thing you can do is let go**, trusting that freedom, both yours and theirs, matters more than appearances.

It takes courage to question the stories you have always been told. Walking away from what dims you is not failure. It is self-validation in action. Some doors are meant to close so you can walk yourself home.

Soul note

Let go of endless striving

Reflect

We're taught that effort makes everything worthwhile. But when trying harder means silencing your needs or abandoning your truth, it stops being noble. It just becomes exhausting. Take a moment to notice if effort has started to cost you more than it gives back.

Try this

Set a timer for ten minutes and write: "What has it cost me to keep trying when something was no longer working?" Let your words flow without filtering or fixing. You don't need to explain or justify. Just let the truth surface.

Mantra

Letting go is not failure. I release the need to fix what's no longer mine to carry. I am learning to trust what unfolds when I stop forcing what won't fit.

Self-soothing dialogue

I don't have to keep pushing just to prove I was loyal or good. I've already given so much. It's okay to stop now. I'm allowed to protect my energy and step back. Letting go doesn't mean I failed. It means I'm finally listening to myself.

Grounding practice

Wrap yourself in a soft blanket or weighted throw. As you breathe in, notice the comfort and support. As you breathe out, picture the pressure to strive leaving your body. Let yourself feel the quiet relief of not having to prove anything right now.

Shared truth

 One of the most courageous decisions you'll ever make is finally letting go of what is hurting your heart and soul."

— BRIGITTE NICOLE

6

MYTH OF HAPPILY EVER AFTER

> The fairytale promise of *"happily ever after"* is more than misleading; it reduces the complexity of love and growth to a static fantasy.

This myth suggests that finding the right person guarantees perpetual happiness, as if love alone can suspend the natural evolution of two distinct souls.

Life paths, like rivers, may run parallel for a time, merge briefly, or diverge toward different horizons, each course shaped by the landscape of our evolving selves. The person who perfectly complemented your journey at twenty-five may no longer align with your path at forty. This is not a failure of love, but the natural outcome of authentic personal growth.

Cultural narratives insist that true love endures unchanged, that with enough compromise and dedication, two people can maintain perfect synchronicity forever. Yet personal growth rarely follows such convenient patterns. When we pledge *"forever,"* we are often promising to remain unchanged, or to change only in ways that preserve the relationship's status quo.

The cost of maintaining this myth is often the gradual abandonment of our internal compass, sacrificing individual truth for the illusion of perpetual harmony. In clinging to this ideal, we risk silencing our own needs, mistaking the quiet of self-abandonment for genuine peace.

> The most genuine relationships are not those that last forever, but those that honour the authentic growth of both individuals, even if that means loving someone enough to release them when paths naturally diverge. **Sometimes, the most profound act of love is the courage to let go,** allowing both people to continue their journey with integrity, rather than forcing a connection that no longer serves either soul's highest truth.

Soul note

Redefining happiness

Reflect

The story of "happily ever after" tells us that love should last forever, no matter what. But real life is more honest than that. Sometimes, love grows and shifts. Sometimes, it ends with grace instead of failure. Think about where you may have mistaken longevity for success, and what it may have cost to keep holding on.

Try this

Think of a version of happiness you used to believe in: a picture-perfect ending, a timeline you thought you should follow, or a role you felt you had to play. Write it down. Then, beneath it, write a new truth that feels more honest for who you are today.

Mantra

I do not owe permanence to the parts of me that have outgrown the fairytale.

Self-soothing dialogue

It's okay that something once felt like forever. It's okay that it didn't last. I'm not breaking a promise by growing. I'm honouring who I really am now. I don't need to shrink to keep old dreams alive. I'm allowed to write a new ending, one that fits me better.

Grounding practice

Warm some lotion or oil in your hands. As you slowly massage your palms and fingers, say, "I honour my growth." Let this simple act become a quiet ritual, a way to remind your body that change is allowed, and you are allowed to evolve too.

Shared truth

> *And they lived happily (aside from a few normal disagreements, misunderstandings, pouts, silent treatments, and unexpected calamities) ever after."*
>
> — JEAN FERRIS, TWICE UPON A MARIGOLD

> *While there is plenty of science to back up the benefits of being in a relationship, being in an unhealthy, toxic, depressing, or divorce-doomed relationship is worse for both your mind and body."*
>
> — LAUREL HOUSE

> *If loving you means abandoning myself, then what we call love is just mutual imprisonment. True devotion doesn't ask us to make ourselves smaller; it invites us both to grow into our fullness.*
>
> — JACE STERLING

7
SOULMATES FOR SALE

Modern culture has taken the ancient idea of soulful connection and packaged it for mass consumption. From glossy memes to viral twin flame readings, the concept of *"the One"* is often sold as a spiritual finish line: an ultimate reward for doing the inner work or finally being *"ready."*

But this marketable version of destiny often distorts more than it delivers. It tells us that our lives are incomplete without a singular soulmate, and that suffering, confusion, or emotional chaos are signs that we're in a divine union rather than red flags that deserve attention.

Yes, genuine soul connections exist. But they don't always arrive wrapped in certainty or lifelong promises. And they are not here to complete us. When we reduce love to a search for "the One," we risk ignoring incompatibility, tolerating pain, and mistaking longing for spiritual depth. Relationships become assignments to decode instead of experiences to inhabit.

The truth? Your soul is not here to find its other half. It's here to evolve. And sometimes the most transformative connections are the ones that teach us when to let go, not just when to hold on.

When you release the pressure to find a partner with cosmic credentials, love becomes something simpler, more honest. It becomes less about fate and more about choice. Connection doesn't need branding. And your life, purpose, and journey hold meaning, with or without a partner.

Lived insight

A couple of years after my separation, I noticed a quiet ache for connection, surfacing in fleeting crushes, imagined futures, and old memories. I mistook it for readiness, but it was a longing to be chosen, to feel needed again.

Recognising this truth did not bring instant relief. It took months to stop scanning for signs, to reroute conversations, to resist reaching out to the past. The search had soothed some uncertainty, but it also kept alive the hope that someone perfect might arrive and restore a sense of belonging. Letting go meant sitting in the silence I once avoided. In that stillness, I began to reclaim myself and began cultivating a quiet and lasting peace.

Soul note

Beyond the illusion of "the one"

Reflect

What if you've never been incomplete? The longing for "the One" often reflects how we've been taught to define love, not what's truly missing. When did connection become something to manifest, prove, or earn?

Try this

Make a short list of beliefs you've held about soulmates or 'the One.' Where did each one come from? A movie? A family story? A spiritual community? Cross out anything that no longer feels true. Circle what still holds meaning.

Mantra

I am the soulmate I most need to connect with.

Self-soothing dialogue

I don't need someone to be my mirror in order to know myself. I am not waiting to be rescued, activated, or completed. Love may still arrive, and I welcome it, but I no longer confuse longing with destiny. I trust the pace and path of my own becoming.

Grounding practice

Play a short piece of calming music or nature sounds. Close your eyes and let the sound fill you. When the track ends, repeat your affirmation: "I am already connected." Let the resonance replace the search.

Shared truth

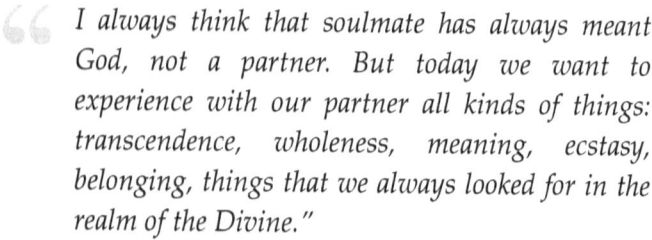

> *I always think that soulmate has always meant God, not a partner. But today we want to experience with our partner all kinds of things: transcendence, wholeness, meaning, ecstasy, belonging, things that we always looked for in the realm of the Divine."*

— ESTHER PEREL

Soulmate concepts

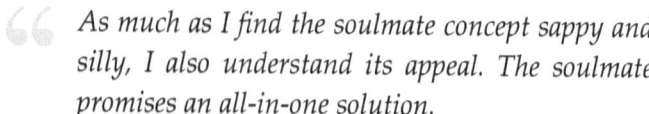

> *As much as I find the soulmate concept sappy and silly, I also understand its appeal. The soulmate promises an all-in-one solution.*
>
> *"Find that one perfect person and you have—for starters—your best friend, your sexual partner, your comforter and caretaker, your cheerleader, your escort to every social function, your consultant on matters large and small, and the one*

and only teammate you will ever need in home management, money management, and vacation planning. And that list doesn't even include any of the potential co- parenting possibilities.

"The soulmate mythology is the ultimate seduction: Find that one right person and all of your wishes will come true."

— BELLA DEPAULO PH.D., SINGLED OUT: HOW SINGLES ARE STEREOTYPED, STIGMATIZED, AND IGNORED, AND STILL LIVE HAPPILY EVER AFTER

The soulmate myth asserts that someone out there is destined to complete you.

"If I believed in soulmates at all, it would be this: someone whose presence helps you remember your own path, not abandon it.

"Someone who amplifies your frequency, not because they are the same, but because your differences call you more deeply into alignment with your own truth."

— JACE STERLING

8

ALONE IS NOT THE PROBLEM

Solitude's most profound gift is the rediscovery of your inner voice, quiet wisdom often silenced by the demands of partnership. In challenging relationships, we learn to mute our internal compass, dimming our truth to maintain an illusion of harmony.

At first, this voice may erupt as a storm, years of unacknowledged needs, buried fears, and forgotten dreams clamouring to be heard. The initial upheaval can feel overwhelming, but gradually, like waves settling after a gale, the noise gives way to clarity.

As you learn to love being alone, you develop an intimate dialogue with your own inner knowing. What begins as tentative acknowledgment blossoms into sacred understanding. You learn to distinguish fear-based thoughts from those guided by intuition. The static of external expectation fades, making space for authentic wisdom to emerge.

This is the power of conscious solitude:
>reclaiming your ability to hear and honour your deepest truth.

Your inner voice becomes your most trusted guide, leading you toward authentic living, both in solitude and in connection with others.

Learning to make the most of the times you spend with yourself is not about feeling deprived or forcing yourself to embrace loneliness. It is about stepping away from external distraction, validation, and attachment so you can reconnect with and validate your deepest, long-neglected needs.

Solitude becomes a journey of self-acceptance, an invitation to welcome home the parts of yourself that once hid in the shadows.

Soul note

Finding peace in solitude

Reflect

Being alone is not the same as being lost. Sometimes, solitude is the only space quiet enough for your peace to return. When the world stops asking who you should be, your own voice begins to remind you who you already are. Let yourself listen.

Try this

Find a quiet space and set a timer for five minutes. Place your hand over your heart or rest it gently on your belly. Ask, "What do I need right now that only I can give myself?" Let the answer rise slowly, like breath. Whatever comes, even if it surprises you, write it down.

Mantra

Solitude is not my lack. It is my listening space.

Self-soothing dialogue

It's okay if this feels strange. I've spent a long time tuning out my own voice. But I'm here now, and I'm listening. I don't need to rush. I don't need to have the answers. I just need to keep showing up for myself. That's enough.

Grounding practice

Sit by a window or step outside if you can. Notice one thing in the natural world: the sky, the movement of leaves, the scent of air, or the warmth or coolness on your skin. Take three deep breaths. With each exhale, quietly say, "I belong to this moment." Let nature remind you that you are held and that calm is possible.

Shared truth

 Knowing how to be solitary is central to the art of loving. When we can be alone, we can be with others without using them as a means of escape."

— BELL HOOKS, FROM ALL ABOUT LOVE: NEW VISIONS (2000)

When loneliness storms through

In the rawness of solitude, especially after loss, emotions surge like waves. Our instinct is often to run from the storm, to fill the empty spaces with noise, distraction, or hasty new connections. Yet there is profound courage in staying present with discomfort.

This pain is not punishment. It is a testament to your capacity for deep feeling. You are not broken; you are breaking open, making space for new growth.

Remember: This storm will pass. The intensity of these emotions will settle into gentle ripples of memory. Nothing has permanently broken you. Give time the chance to teach you how to heal.

A season of loneliness and isolation is when the caterpillar gets its wings. Remember that next time you feel alone."

— MANY HALE, THE SINGLE WOMAN: LIFE, LOVE, AND A DASH OF SASS

Sacred gifts of embracing solitude

Your inner voice awakens: Free from external noise, your intuition and wisdom become clear, trusted guides for life's choices.

Peace becomes your natural state: Your mind quiets, revealing a deep stability that flows from within rather than from external validation.

Self-trust takes root: You honour your instincts and make decisions aligned with your truth, not others' expectations.

Boundaries flow naturally: Understanding your own needs becomes second nature, creating space for authentic relationships instead of obligations.

Time becomes sacred: Each moment holds the potential for joy, from morning rituals to evening reflections, all experienced fully on your terms.

Authenticity emerges effortlessly: Without the pressure to perform or please, your true self unfolds naturally and takes centre stage.

Self-love deepens into wisdom: What begins as accepting your own company evolves into a profound understanding of your worth and inherent completeness.

9

RELEASING EXTERNAL VALIDATION

From a young age, we are conditioned to seek approval and acceptance from those around us. The implicit message is clear: to be safe, we must conform to the expectations of our "tribe": family, school, religion, or the broader social fabric. We learn to mould ourselves into what we believe will earn us the validation and belonging we crave.

This deep-seated need for external approval often becomes so ingrained that it quietly follows us into adulthood as a persistent quest for validation.

The gift of singlehood, or periods of solitude, is the opportunity to reevaluate what feels genuinely meaningful, beyond the expectations of others. Without the constant pressures of performative relating, we can peel back the layers of conditioning and societal programming.

Letting go of the need for external validation

means discerning which feedback serves our growth, and which expectations we can consciously release.

It is the practice of cultivating self-trust, allowing ourselves to live in alignment with our inner essence.

Soul note

Living true to yourself

Reflect

Approval often felt like safety growing up. Without the constant mirror of others' feedback, you can ask: "Who am I when I stop performing?"

Try this

Think of one "should" belief about who you are. Where did it come from? Ask if it still serves you. Write your response somewhere you'll see it.

Mantra

I am allowed to evolve, change, and redefine myself. I do not need permission to express what's real for me. Each day, I practice returning to what feels true, even as it changes.

Self-soothing dialogue

It's okay if this feels unfamiliar. I've spent a long time trying to meet others' expectations. But now, I choose to listen to my own voice. I don't need to prove my worth, I am already enough. I trust myself to make choices that honour who I truly am.

Grounding practice

Place a drop of calming essential oil (like lavender or chamomile) on your wrist or a tissue. Inhale deeply. As you exhale, quietly say: "I am already enough." Let this scent anchor you in your own presence.

Shared truth

> *To be yourself in a world that is constantly trying to make you something else is the greatest accomplishment."*
>
> — RALPH WALDO EMERSON

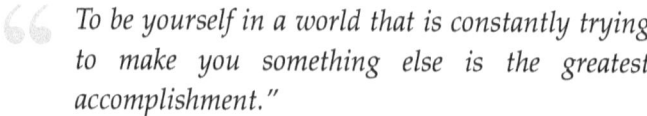

> *Stay true to yourself. An original is worth more than a copy."*
>
> — SUZY KASSEM

> *Sometimes, when you think you've hit rock bottom, what you've really hit is the foundation for the next chapter in your life."*
>
> — MEGHAN QUINN

> *You can't start the next chapter of your life if you keep re-reading the last one."*
>
> — MICHAEL MCMILLAN

10

SAYING NO WITHOUT LOSING YOURSELF

Saying *"no"* is more than basic boundary-setting. While many focus on surface-level techniques, the real work lies in transforming refusal from a defensive reaction into an expression of profound self-trust. Each time you decline a request, change your mind, or stand firm, you reveal who you are and what you value.

Consider how certain patterns might undermine your integrity: ghosting commitments when overwhelmed, using *"no"* to punish those who have hurt you, or creating elaborate excuses instead of speaking the truth. These habits may temporarily avoid conflict, but ultimately, they erode trust both in relationships and within yourself.

> **Your intuition deserves profound respect.** It is your inner compass, signalling when something does not align, and that alone is reason enough to say no.

Declining something simply because it does not feel right requires no elaborate justification. Yet this freedom to honour your truth comes with responsibility. When circumstances shift after you have committed, early communication preserves trust and respect.

The skill develops through conscious practice: requesting refunds when warranted, negotiating for what you need, or standing firm when facing disapproval. Each authentic refusal strengthens your reliability. Your *"no"* gains power not through harshness, but through the consistency between your words and actions.

Some relationships will challenge your growth toward honest communication. Friends accustomed to your automatic *"yes"* may resist this change, interpreting your boundaries as rejection. This discomfort signals transformation. You are replacing people-pleasing with genuine connection based on mutual respect.

Every authentic *"no"* reflects your commitment to integrity. Each refusal strengthens your foundation of trust, creating space for the deeper, more meaningful connections you deserve.

Lived insight

I used to believe that kindness meant always saying yes, especially when I had more to give than someone else. I learned early that love was measured in sacrifice. My mum rarely put herself first, and my dad helped others without hesitation. I followed suit, barely pausing to consider my own limits. Whether it was money, time, or emotional labour, I gave freely, even when it left me stretched thin and quietly overwhelmed. For years, I wore reliability like a badge of honour.

> Sometimes I sensed the imbalance, but I dismissed it, convinced that being generous was just what love should look like. But I wasn't honest with myself about what it truly cost. Looking back, I see how easily others came to rely on my help, often without much thought for giving anything in return. I was always dependable, but when I needed support, many simply stepped back. My giving wasn't always about love. It was also, sometimes, about staying needed and connected, even if it meant losing myself a little more each time.

The real change came when I started saying no, not out of anger but from a place of self-respect. That was when I saw that the foundation of some relationships was not love, but access. Saying no hasn't always felt comfortable, but it has revealed who sees me as a whole person, not just as someone useful. Now, I look for connection where my needs are seen and don't require justification. My boundaries are not warnings. They are an honest part of who I am, and if someone can't meet me there, I let go, knowing that my peace and self-respect stay with me.

Soul note

Integrity through honest no's

Reflect

Saying no is not a failure of kindness. It is an act of self-alignment. If you've spent years being agreeable or helpful, your yes may have become automatic, even at your own expense. Each time you override your inner knowing to keep the peace, you chip away at self-trust. What if saying no isn't about rejection, but about restoring your relationship with yourself?

Try this

Think of a recent moment when you agreed to something but wanted to say no. Quietly replay it in your mind. What held you back from speaking your truth? Write the sentence you wish you had said: simple, clear, and honest. Let this become your starting point for practicing aligned refusal.

Mantra

My no is just as sacred as my yes. I say yes to myself without guilt or shame.

Self-soothing dialogue

I am not unkind for saying no. I am not difficult for setting limits. I can be clear and still be compassionate.

Honouring what feels true protects my energy and helps my relationships stay honest. I do not need to justify every no. I only need to trust myself to mean what I say.

Grounding practice

Stand and slowly stretch your arms out to each side, forming a circle of space around you. As you breathe, imagine this space as your boundary: safe, clear, and respected. Let your body remember how it feels to honour your limits.

Shared truth

> *Boundaries are the distance at which I can love you and me simultaneously."*
>
> — PRENTIS HEMPHILL

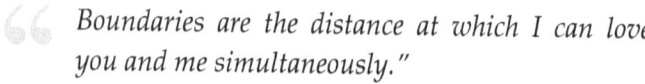

> *When you say yes to others, make sure you are not saying no to yourself."*
>
> — PAULO COELHO

11

ENERGY EXCHANGE: PATTERN RESET

Have you noticed how certain people leave you feeling inexplicably drained, while others energise your spirit? These reactions reveal important truths about the balance of energy in your relationships. Every interaction carries an exchange of emotional labour, attention, and care.

> **When giving depletes you entirely, it is not generosity but self-abandonment.**

Our patterns of giving and receiving often stem from early survival strategies. Many take pride in being natural givers, but this pattern often masks hyper vigilant coping mechanisms shaped by environments where peace depended on meeting others' needs. Similarly, those who became comfortable receiving without recognising its cost may unconsciously equate others' giving with proof of worth. Both positions create relationships founded on depletion rather than mutual growth.

These dynamics extend beyond romantic partnerships into every connection we maintain.

> Healthy relationships thrive on mindful exchange, not the quiet erosion of one person's boundaries.

The exhaustion that follows these imbalanced exchanges is not just fatigue; it is your body signalling that something fundamental needs to shift in how you engage with others.

Reflect: Are you giving to feel safe, to earn love, or out of habit? Are you taking without awareness of the care behind it, or assuming it as proof of your worth? The way you exchange energy reveals not just how you connect with others, but how you honour your own needs.

By recognising these patterns, we create space for connections grounded in mutual respect, where giving and receiving become acts of choice, not obligation.

Soul note

Balance the give and take

Reflect

Not all generosity is selfless. Sometimes, giving is a way to feel safe, needed, or worthy. These patterns often echo old survival strategies, such as hyper-attunement or avoidance from our earliest relationships. Notice where your giving feels expansive, and where it leaves you depleted. Where in your life is giving costing more than it restores?

Try this

For one day, keep an "energy ledger." On the left, list any interactions that left you feeling drained. On the right, note those that felt energising or mutual. No need to fix anything. Just observe the balance. What patterns do you notice?

Mantra

I allow myself to give and receive, knowing both are required to create universal balance and flow.

Self-soothing dialogue

I am not here to rescue or over-function. My care matters, but so do my limits. I can step back without guilt. My presence is not a resource to be managed by others. It is a gift I choose when it feels right.

Grounding practice

Sit quietly with a warm object, such as a cup of tea, a heated pack, or your hands cupped together. Let the warmth remind you that energy flows best when it is contained and replenished. Say quietly, "I can hold warmth without spilling it all away."

Shared truth

> *True generosity is not measured by how much you give, but by how little you betray yourself in the process."*
>
> — ANONYMOUS

> *Don't set yourself on fire trying to keep others warm."*
>
> — PENNY REID

> *The best relationships are built on mutual care and shared accountability for the energy exchanged."*
>
> — UNKNOWN

> *Givers need to set limits because takers rarely do."*
>
> — RACHEL WOLCHIN

> *Healing comes when we recognise that no one can give us what we haven't given ourselves."*
>
> — UNKNOWN

12

STOP RUSHING BACK TO LOVE

The rush to find new love often masks a deeper fear: the fear of sitting with ourselves in the quiet aftermath of endings. This urgency to partner again is not merely about companionship; it may be an attempt to outrun the essential work of healing and self-discovery that solitude offers.

When we leap too quickly into new relationships, we carry forward not just our unfulfilled hopes but our unexamined patterns and unhealed hurts. Like applying a bandage before properly cleaning a wound, hasty partnerships often cover rather than heal the deeper needs that require attention. This temporary fix can lead to repeating the very relationship dynamics we are trying to escape.

> **The space between relationships is not a void to fill, but an invitation to reclaim your relationship with yourself.** In this sacred

pause, you can examine your patterns, strengthen your boundaries, and cultivate the kind of self-knowledge that makes future partnerships choices rather than necessities.

True readiness for love comes not from fearing solitude, but from deeply understanding yourself. This understanding allows you to intentionally and selectively choose who enters your life, grounded in a healed, heart-centred space.

> Intentional singlehood is not just about healing; it is about rediscovering who you are when you are no longer defining yourself through someone else's eyes.

Soul note

Don't rush the rebuild

Reflect

The instinct to rush back into love can feel like momentum, but often it's avoidance in disguise. Underneath the urgency to connect may be fear: fear of loneliness, of stillness, of sitting in the quiet with unmet needs. But solitude is not a setback. It's the space where your foundation is rebuilt, stronger, steadier, and more true to who you are. What part of yourself is asking to be rebuilt before you let someone new in?

Try this

Choose one small social or romantic interaction, such as responding to a message, saying yes to a date, or initiating contact, and delay your response by 24 hours. During that pause, write down any emotions or sensations that arise. Are you reaching out from curiosity, connection, or discomfort? Use this pause as a mirror, not a test.

Mantra

I honour my own pace.

Self-soothing dialogue

I am not behind. I am rebuilding something real. It's okay if it takes time. Wholeness is not measured by how quickly I move on. It is measured by how honestly I come back to myself. This space I am in is not empty. It is a time of becoming.

Grounding practice

Sip a warm cup of tea or broth slowly, with both hands wrapped around the cup. Feel the warmth travel into your chest and belly. Let the slow pace of this ritual remind you that not all things need to happen quickly to be meaningful.

Shared truth

 You are not a project that needs to be hurried through. You are a season worth experiencing slowly."

— ANONYMOUS

Signs you're not ready to date again

If any of these resonate, it may be a sign to pause and focus on your own healing before pursuing new connections.

- You have not processed past pain.
- You are seeking someone to *"choose"* or *"find"* you.
- You feel uncomfortable being alone.
- You view relationships as the solution to your problems.
- You remain stuck in unhealthy patterns.
- You find yourself drawn to the same harmful dynamics or personalities.
- Your boundaries are unclear or inconsistent.
- You idealise people you have just met.
- You obsess over finding a *"twin flame"* or *"soulmate."*

Healed signs vs. signs of limerence

- **Grounded in reality:** Fantasises about unrealistic scenarios
- **Respects personal boundaries:** Obsessively seeks validation or attention
- **Values slow, steady connection:** Rushed emotional intensity
- **Feels emotionally balanced:** Experiences extreme emotional highs/lows
- **Seeks mutual understanding:** Focuses on imagined traits of the other
- **Accepts outcomes without attachment:** Fearful of rejection or loss
- **Enjoys independence:** Constant need for proximity or contact
- **Enjoys present-moment connection:** Preoccupied with future fantasies or "what ifs"
- **Open to reciprocal vulnerability:** Afraid to reveal true self, idealises from a distance

---

If you don't heal what hurt you, you'll bleed on people who didn't cut you."

— UNKNOWN

When the stories of our life no longer bind us, we discover within them something greater. We discover that within the very limitations of form

... of parenthood and childhood ... of gravity on the earth and the changing of the seasons, is the freedom and harmony we have sought for so long. Our individual life is an expression of the whole mystery, and in it we can rest in the center of the movement, the center of all worlds."

— JACK KORNFIELD

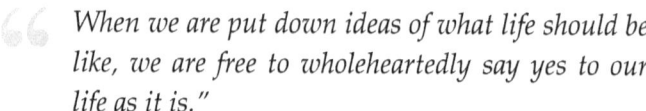

When we are put down ideas of what life should be like, we are free to wholeheartedly say yes to our life as it is."

— TARA BACH

13

IT'S A PATTERN, NOT LOVE!

> Beneath every relationship choice is a web of unconscious patterns: habits that quietly shape our attractions, reactions, and attachments.

These invisible architects guide our experiences long before we recognise their influence.

Like well-worn paths in a forest, these patterns often begin as tentative steps taken in response to early experiences of love, loss, or protection. Over time, they harden into familiar routes, leading us repeatedly toward the same dynamics, regardless of whether they serve our growth. We find ourselves drawn to certain types of people, replaying similar scenarios, wondering why the script feels so predictable.

Each relationship becomes a mirror, reflecting these hidden patterns through emotional triggers, communication styles, and unspoken expectations. We might seek validation from unavailable partners, build walls that block genuine connection, or swing between craving closeness and fiercely guarding our autonomy, never quite finding ease in authentic intimacy.

> **Recognising these patterns is not a condemnation.** It is an invitation to meet ourselves with honesty and compassion, and to choose a new way forward.

Rather than judging these habits as flaws, we can understand them as outdated protection mechanisms, crafted from times when love was uncertain or inconsistent. They were built to keep us safe. Now, they are ready for renewal.

By bringing conscious attention to these automatic responses, we carve new paths: ones that no longer circle back to familiar disappointment, but lead toward authentic connection with ourselves and others.

Soul note

Beyond familiar paths

Reflect

Some patterns look like love because they once felt like safety. Even when they hurt, they're familiar, and familiarity can feel like truth. But predictable pain is not connection. Notice what feels automatic in your relational responses. Do you chase, retreat, or repeat? These patterns were once protection. Now, they might be keeping you from what you truly need.

Try this

Draw a simple diagram or flowchart of a relationship pattern you want to break. Start with a trigger or dynamic (e.g., "I feel ignored") and follow the usual sequence of thoughts, reactions, and behaviours that unfold. Then, sketch an alternative path you'd like to try. You don't need to act on it yet. Just seeing the loop clearly is a powerful shift.

Mantra

I am free to choose new patterns.

Self-soothing dialogue

These old habits helped me survive uncertain love. They were never about weakness; they were built from care, vigilance, and a desire to belong. But I don't need to live on repeat. I can value where I've been and still step toward something new.

Grounding practice

With one finger, gently trace a spiral on the palm of your opposite hand. Let the motion be slow and intentional. As you move inward, say quietly, "I see the pattern." As you move outward, say, "I choose a new path." Repeat as often as needed until your nervous system softens.

Shared truth

> *Sometimes what feels like love or attraction is just a familiar pattern trying to repeat itself."*
>
> — JACE STERLING

> *If you're working on changing bad habits, unhealthy thought patterns, negative emotions, or toxic behaviours, know that you are healing a small part of the world by healing yourself.*
>
> *"Everyone around you will benefit, and they will be served by your wholeness. It's hard sometimes, and I know you want to quit, but this is the work that ultimately changes the world."*
>
> — EMILY MAROUTIAN

> *The truth is, unless you let go, unless you forgive yourself, unless you forgive the situation, unless you realise that the situation is over, you cannot move forward. "*
>
> — STEVE MARABOLI

14

FINDING YOUR STRENGTH

Society delights in categorising single people, attaching assumptions to every label: career devotee, eternal romantic, independent spirit. Yet these labels often conceal the deeper truths of living life on one's own terms.

What others perceive as limitations or circumstantial choices often contain hidden strengths. Not mythic resilience or compensatory gifts, but quiet capabilities that emerge through navigating life's challenges independently. The single parent's resourcefulness, the widow's resilience, the solo dweller's self-sufficiency: these are not badges of honour, but practical adaptations, skills honed by meeting life's demands without the scaffold of partnership.

This is not to suggest that those with more resources or shared responsibilities develop less character. Partnership fosters growth in its own way. Yet singlehood brings a unique opportunity to cultivate self-reliance, asking us to manage finances, create homes, build support networks, and plan futures without relying on the traditional structures of partnership. These responsibilities shape us in ways that transcend the stereotypes society imposes.

Sometimes it takes losing the life we planned to find the self we were meant to become. True strength rarely arrives through dramatic victories. It takes shape in the quiet moments: rising each day, holding a boundary, reaching out for help. These are the steady efforts that reveal our resilience, often long before we recognise it.

The journey of singlehood, in all its varied forms, often leads to a profound understanding of resilience. Not because singlehood automatically makes us stronger, but because facing life's complexities primarily on our own terms reveals strengths we might never have discovered in more dependent dynamics. In discovering these strengths, we move beyond society's categories and into the quiet power of our own becoming.

Soul note

The strength no one saw

Reflect

Strength doesn't always look like what people expect. It isn't loud, visible, or celebrated. Sometimes, it's doing the grocery run alone after a hard day. Sometimes, it's asking for help when you'd rather not. The world may not notice these moments, but they count. They are the shape of a self that keeps showing up, quietly proving it can.

Try this

List three moments from your past where you handled something on your own. Not the big life events, just the everyday difficulties that required courage, creativity, or persistence. Write down what quality in you made that possible. Name it.

Mantra

My strength grows from within.

Self-soothing dialogue

Some days were just hard, but I got through them, even if it wasn't pretty. I don't have to look strong for it to count. Quiet effort matters. I'm starting to see the strength in just showing up, even when nobody else sees it.

Grounding practice

Stand tall with your feet shoulder-width apart. Let your arms rest by your side or on your hips. Breathe deeply into your belly and say to yourself, "I'm here. I'm strong. I'm still standing." Hold the posture for 60 seconds.

Shared truth

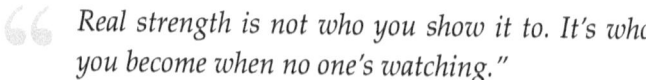 *Real strength is not who you show it to. It's who you become when no one's watching."*

— ANONYMOUS

15

HOW WE SAY GOODBYE MATTERS

In the aftermath of separation, it is natural to armour ourselves with judgment and resentment. The mind constructs elaborate narratives of blame, replaying moments of hurt and betrayal in an endless loop of self-justification. Yet this protective shell, meant to guard against further pain, often becomes a prison that blocks our healing and growth.

Compassion offers a different path. Not passive acceptance or denial of legitimate grievances, but a conscious liberation from the weight of sustained anger. **Holding onto resentment binds us more tightly to past hurts than any external circumstance ever could.**

This shift requires courage, especially as time passes and the landscape of separation begins to change. Even the most amicable arrangements can evolve. New relationships, shifting loyalties, or the slow surfacing of old wounds can alter the tone of communication and the boundaries you once took for granted. What began in mutual goodwill may, over months or years, give way to defensiveness, withdrawal, or subtle forms of competition. These changes are not always rooted in malice. More often, they reflect the discomfort of growth, the limits of another's capacity, or the emergence of patterns that were once dormant.

You may find yourself surprised, even hurt, by how much someone changes after separation. But resist the temptation to see every shift as a personal failure. It's easy to take rejection or disrespect from someone you once loved as something to do with you, but often their behaviour is projection, an unwillingness to face their own healing work.

> These moments are echoes, invitations to notice whether you have changed and truly disengaged.

They are signals, reminders to reassess your expectations and reinforce your own emotional boundaries. Your responsibility is not to manage someone else's evolution. It is to stay anchored in your own.

Letting go is not a single event. It happens in stages. Early on, you may find yourself consumed by logistics, grief, and negotiations. Later, the work becomes more internal: releasing old roles, disentangling identities, and unlearning habits of emotional over- functioning. Eventually, it becomes about reducing the energetic and psychological overlap that ties you to outdated dynamics.

> The relationship may have ended, but its emotional infrastructure often lingers until you consciously dismantle it.

This is especially true for those navigating shared parenting or financial complexities. A second wave of separation often arrives quietly, when someone remarries, when a financial agreement unravels, or when co-parenting expectations shift without warning. These changes can be disorienting. But they are not regressions. They are invitations to revisit your values, reinforce your boundaries, and accept that your path and theirs may no longer align, even in the name of peace.

Give yourself permission to disconnect. Stop following your ex on social media. Limit conversations to what is necessary. Release the need for validation from someone who may no longer be able to offer it. This is not spite. It is self-preservation.

> Boundaries are quiet recalibrations, not acts of aggression. Compassion sometimes means choosing distance and allowing healing to unfold.

As you evolve, some people will resist that change, especially if they once benefited from the version of you who stayed small, agreeable, or emotionally available at all costs. Their disappointment is not a reliable measure of your integrity. What others label as disappointment is often conditional approval, control, or discomfort dressed as concern. Growth can unsettle relationships built on self-abandonment. Expect to disappoint people if you've spent a lifetime trying to please them. Expect pushback if you begin to assert new values, new limits, or a new voice. The task is not to please. **The task is to stay present and rooted in who you are becoming.**

> The universe loans people to us for moments or lifetimes, but none are truly ours to keep. We are not here to manage how others perceive our evolution. We are here to learn how to stand inside it with integrity. Sometimes the deepest form of love is letting go without animosity. Let the past close gently so your future can begin.

As you navigate your own goodbyes, notice where old patterns tug at your attention. What are you being asked to release? What new boundaries does this season require? Trust that letting go, though rarely comfortable, is often the most courageous form of self-respect.

Lived insight

Accepting that not every connection is meant to last forever requires a particular kind of courage. When I look back across my life and all my past relationships, I can see a pattern of enmeshment, some form of codependency, whether overt or subtle. Some were less toxic than others, but in all of them, I gradually lost touch with myself. This disconnection showed up in many ways: sometimes as depression, other times as physical illness, stress, weight gain, or a quiet sense of emptiness and self-abandonment. The truth is, I hadn't yet learned the delicate skill of loving another while keeping hold of my own identity, needs, and boundaries. I only knew how to dissolve into love, how to make someone else's happiness my centre of gravity.

> Breaking free from those patterns, one goodbye at a time, became the beginning of real self-recognition. A quiet sense of rightness would wash over me every time I chose myself again.

Reclaiming my identity and my needs wasn't selfish. It was necessary. Each ending, though painful, became an act of self-validation and a doorway back to wholeness.

Saying goodbye asked me to bear witness to truth, not just sentiment. Whenever I felt tempted to look back, I reread the reasons I needed to go. That list became my anchor, steadying me when memories, sentiment, guilt, or obligation tried to rewrite the past.

> The truth is, endings rarely feel clean or cinematic. They bring disruption, turmoil, doubt, grief, and confusion. I didn't just grieve the person I loved; I found myself grieving the person I might have been, and the time I lost loving someone who wasn't right for my future.

The contrast between who I was when I fell in love and

who I became over time was sometimes stark, and facing that truth was both confronting and clarifying.

In those moments, the inner battle intensified. Self-doubt made me question my motives and my reality. But in time, and with conscious, repeated effort, I learned how to step out of the arena, to silence the war within long enough to connect with my inner truth and deliberately end old cycles. That is the real work of goodbye: not just letting go of another, but reclaiming myself in the aftermath, with all the mess and wisdom that process brings.

Soul notes

Saying goodbye without staying stuck

Reflect

Letting go is rarely neat. After a separation, the mind often replays old arguments and aches for closure that may never come. Saying goodbye is more than walking away. It's choosing not to let the past dictate your peace. You can acknowledge what happened without carrying it into every quiet moment. What would it mean to release this, for your own sake?

Try this

Recall a recent moment when you set a boundary. Write a version of that "no" that is simple, kind, and clear. You don't need to send it. This is about practicing self-respect and letting your needs guide your goodbye.

Mantra

Grace and boundaries can coexist.

Self-soothing dialogue

I'm allowed to protect my peace, even if others don't understand. I can be kind and still choose to walk away. I don't have to give more of myself just to make things easier for someone else. I've spent enough time justifying my choices. Letting go isn't selfish. It's me being honest about what I need in order to move forward. I can choose clarity instead of guilt. I can choose quiet instead of chaos. I'm allowed to let things end, even if someone else wishes they wouldn't.

Grounding practice

Hold a smooth stone, piece of fabric, or other small object in your hand. Feel its texture and weight as you breathe slowly. With each exhale, imagine any lingering tension leaving your body. Let this simple act remind you: you do not have to carry what is no longer yours.

Shared truth

The only closure you need is the one you give yourself."

— BRIANNA WIEST

We cannot offer others what we deny ourselves. When we withhold compassion, forgiveness, or peace from ourselves, we live by double standards.

"My life only began to align when I interrupted that narrative and allowed myself the same grace and empathy I so freely gave to others."

— JACE STERLING

An important note on safety and separation

This chapter was written from a place of relative safety and mutual respect. I know not all relationships can end this way, and some absolutely should not.

If you are navigating abuse, coercion, or ongoing harm, especially where children are involved, your safety and your children's safety come first. Please do not take this chapter as encouragement to stay in contact or extend empathy in situations that are unsafe.

The invitation here is to explore where kindness, forgiveness, or empathy might support healing, not to assume they always should.

There is no shame in choosing distance or ending contact when that is what safety or self-respect require. Your boundaries, your truth, and your safety matter most.

This chapter offers reflection only. It is not therapeutic or legal advice. If you are in an unsafe situation, please seek guidance from qualified professionals.

> *Out beyond ideas of wrong doing and right doing, there is a field. I'll meet you there."*
>
> — RUMI

> *In the end, only three things matter: how much you loved, how gently you lived, and how gracefully you let go of things not meant for you."*
>
> — BUDDHA

Letting go and self compassion

> *When we let go of our battles and open our heart to things as they are, then we come to rest in the present moment. This is the beginning and the end of spiritual practice. Only in this moment can we discover that which is timeless.*

"Only here can we find the love that we seek. Love in the past is simply memory, and love in the future is fantasy. Only in the reality of the present can we love, can we awaken, can we find peace and understanding and connection with ourselves and the world."

— JACK KORNFIELD, A PATH WITH HEART: A GUIDE THROUGH THE PERILS AND PROMISES OF SPIRITUAL LIFE

16

BUILDING SELF-WORTH

Understanding the difference between self-confidence and self- worth is a quiet revelation. Self-confidence rises and falls with our perceived successes and challenges. It is situational, often tethered to specific abilities or moments. Self-worth, by contrast, is foundational: the unwavering knowing that we are worthy of love and belonging simply because we exist.

Periods of solitude bring this truth into sharper focus. Without the noise of constant validation-seeking, our inner voice grows clearer. We begin to notice the subtle ways we have abandoned our own worth in pursuit of approval, dimming our light to make others more comfortable.

> Building authentic self-worth means consciously releasing the belief that our value must be earned.

It asks us to challenge the internalised messages that tie our worth to achievement, status, or the opinions of others. In this space of reclamation, we discover that what we once labelled as imperfections are, in fact, essential threads in the fabric of our wholeness.

> True self-worth transforms every aspect of life.
> When we know our value at the core, we stop seeking completion through external sources.

We become free to create lives and relationships that honour our worth, rather than define it. This shift is not a single act, but a continuous practice, a gentle, persistent return to ourselves.

In this space of wholeness, we become architects of lives liberated from the need for external validation, building futures that reflect, not determine, our worth.

Soul note

Don't let anyone else define what you're worth

Reflect

Sometimes we confuse self-worth with self-confidence, but they're not the same. Confidence can fade when we fail or feel uncertain. Self-worth doesn't move. It's the quiet knowing that you are enough, even when you feel unsure, even when no one is clapping. Think about the ways you've handed other people the power to measure your worth, through their approval, their opinions, their attention. What would it feel like to take that power back?

Try this

Write a short letter to your younger self. Not to change her path, but to remind her she was always worthy, before the grades, before the relationships, before she tried to earn love. Keep it simple. Let her hear what no one else said enough.

Mantra

I am worthy, always. Even when I feel overlooked or uncertain, my value remains intact. Nothing and no one can alter the truth of my worth.

Self-soothing dialogue

Sometimes I feel out of place. Misunderstood. Like I'm too much, or not quite enough. I've felt overlooked, underestimated, and unsupported; it's easy to start questioning my worth when that happens. But I'm learning that other people's limitations aren't a reflection of my value. I can give myself the understanding I need, even when others can't. I can show up for myself, especially when it matters most. My worth is steady, even when the world is not.

Grounding practice

Stand in front of a mirror. Meet your own gaze without looking away. Place a hand gently on your chest or cheek. Stay with yourself for one full minute. Let this be a quiet reminder: I belong to myself first.

Shared truth

> *I can know my worth and still lack confidence at times. We should not collapse these distinctions."*
>
> — JACE STERLING

> *Self-confidence gives you drive. Self-worth gives you peace. Self confidence is optional. Self-worth is essential. Self-confidence eventually surrenders. Self-worth ultimately prevails."*
>
> — JAMIE KERN LIMA

17

BECOMING ANTI-FRAGILE

While resilience is often praised as the ability to recover from setbacks, a more powerful possibility exists: becoming anti-fragile.

> Philosopher Nassim Nicholas Taleb describes anti-fragility as the capacity not just to withstand stress, but to evolve and grow because of it. This mindset transforms singlehood from something to endure into a catalyst for extraordinary personal evolution.

Those who approach solo living with anti-fragility do not merely survive its challenges. They recognise that responsibility, solitude, and uncertainty are not obstacles to overcome but the very conditions that forge new strengths. Anti-fragility is not about denying pain or maintaining a brave façade. **It is the willingness to fully acknowledge struggle while remaining committed to extracting its transformative potential.**

Every disruption becomes an invitation to expand. Each moment of uncertainty reveals capacities we never knew we possessed. Instead of exhausting ourselves resisting life's natural tensions, we develop trust in our ability to thrive through change, knowing we are enough exactly as we are, even as we continue to evolve.

Small, conscious choices such as inviting feedback, embracing change in routines, and stepping into unfamiliar territory become the quiet training grounds for anti-fragility. Over time, we build not just resilience but a deeper faith in our ability to be strengthened by life rather than diminished by it.

In consciously chosen singlehood, we discover not just who we are but the full extent of who we might become, growing stronger with every challenge we embrace.

Soul note

Strength through adversity

Reflect

Anti-fragility is not just about surviving hardship. It's about evolving through it. Think of a time when you didn't just recover, but emerged wiser, clearer, or more capable. What changed in you because of that disruption? What part of you got stronger?

Try this

Think of a recent challenge or unexpected change. Instead of asking "Why did this happen to me?" write down three ways it stretched or reshaped you for the better. Even if the growth is still in process, name what's beginning to shift.

Mantra

I grow stronger through challenge. Struggles do not break me; they shape me into someone wiser and more capable. I just need to take the next step forward right now.

Self-soothing dialogue

I don't always welcome disruption. It can shake my sense of stability, and sometimes I wish things could just stay calm. But I've learned that I'm capable of adapting. Every difficulty has left something behind: a lesson, a strength, a deeper truth. I don't have to rush to find meaning, but I trust that I will find it. I can meet the moment, even when I feel unsure.

Grounding practice

Step outside or near a window. Place your hand over your heart and take three slow breaths. As you exhale, imagine yourself becoming a little more rooted with each breath. Then gently clench your fists and release them, noticing the shift from tension to ease. Say to yourself, "I bend, but I do not break."

Shared truth

> *In the depth of winter, I finally learned that within me there lay an invincible summer."*
>
> — ALBERT CAMUS

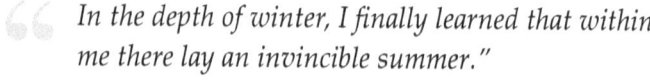

> *Anti-fragility is beyond resilience or robustness. The resilient resists shocks and stays the same; the anti-fragile gets better."*
>
> — NASSIM NICHOLAS TALEB

> *Resilience is not simply about bouncing back. It is about allowing yourself to be shaped, expanded, and strengthened by what once threatened to break you."*
>
> — JACE STERLING

18

WHY WILLPOWER MATTERS

Willpower is often misunderstood as an endless reserve of self- control. In reality, it is a precious resource, one that replenishes with rest and depletes with each decision we make.

> Understanding this pattern changes how we approach self-discipline, especially during seasons of independent living when we alone are responsible for steering our course.

Every choice, from the mundane to the monumental, draws from the same well of mental energy. After a day of navigating challenges and making decisions, it is natural to feel more vulnerable to old habits or the pull of relationships that no longer serve us. This is not a personal failing, but a reflection of how willpower works. Recognising this allows us to respond with self-compassion rather than self-judgment when fatigue sets in.

> The secret is not to strive for superhuman control, but to design an environment and daily rhythm that conserves willpower for what matters most.

By establishing supportive routines and honouring our natural energy cycles, we safeguard this vital resource for choices that truly align with our values and goals. Tackling important tasks earlier in the day, when willpower is highest, helps us move forward with greater clarity and intention.

Preserving willpower is not a sign of weakness or avoidance. It is an act of wise stewardship, ensuring that our limited daily reserves are spent in service of our deepest priorities rather than frittered away by decision fatigue. Structure and habit, not force, become our allies.

As the day progresses and mental energy wanes, be gentle with yourself. Evening cravings for comfort or reconnection are not signs of weakness; they are signals that it is time to rest and restore. Each new day offers a fresh well of resolve. Use it wisely and honour the cycles of effort and renewal that sustain your growth.

Lived insight

For years, I equated every setback in my health with a failure of discipline. I followed rigid routines and endured extended fasts because I believed sheer effort would bring change. Each lapse felt like a personal failing. Only later did I understand how chronic stress and decision fatigue quietly depleted my willpower. If I had known then that willpower was not a test of character, I might have chosen a gentler path.

I still carry echoes of shame, but I am learning to meet those memories with compassion. These days, that looks like resting when I need to, softening my self-talk, and listening to what my body asks for.

This awareness opens a space for genuine empathy toward the woman I once was. She fought so hard to reclaim herself, even when the path felt relentless and overwhelming. I honour her effort and feel deeply relieved to have stepped out of that struggle. The war within has ended, replaced by a quieter freedom and lasting respect for all it took to arrive here.

Soul note

Willpower is a skill, not a test

Reflect

Willpower isn't a character test. It's a battery. Every decision, big or small, draws from the same charge. By evening, it's natural to feel depleted. Think of a time you made a choice you later questioned, not because you didn't care, but because you were tired. It's easy to skip a walk after a long day or to put off the things that once brought you joy, like writing, music, or calling a friend.

Over time, what matters most can quietly slip onto the *"if-only"* or *"one-day"* list. What if, instead of assuming you have failed or lacked discipline, you became curious about why some things feel easier at certain times of the day?

Try this

Begin your day with one meaningful task. Choose something that nurtures your growth, not just your responsibilities. Give your freshest energy to what matters most before the rest of the day starts making demands.

Mantra

I do what matters most when my energy is strongest.

Self-soothing dialogue

Some days I forget that willpower has limits. It's not weakness or laziness. Decision fatigue is real. What I do, and when I do it, matters. I can learn to plan for the times when I'm at my best and give myself grace when I'm not. Not every slip means I've failed. Even knowing what I don't want helps me move toward what I prefer to create. This isn't about trying harder. It's about learning how to set up my life to reduce resistance, so I don't need to force my way through every challenge. I can build these skills. I'm allowed to grow without judgment.

Grounding practice

Hold a warm cup of tea or coffee in your hands. Feel the heat in your palms as you breathe deeply. As you sip, say quietly, "I begin with what matters." Let this small ritual mark the start of a day shaped by intention.

Shared truth

> *Sometimes it looks like people with great self-control aren't working hard, but that's because they've made it automatic."*
>
> — ANGELA DUCKWORTH

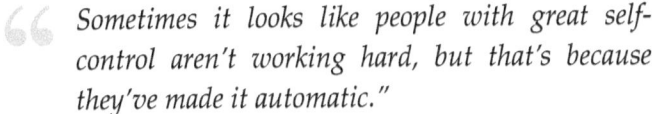

> *The link between willpower and decision-making works both ways: Decision-making depletes your willpower, and once your willpower is depleted, you're less able to make decisions."*
>
> — ROY F. BAUMEISTER & JOHN TIERNY,
> WILLPOWER: REDISCOVERING THE
> GREATEST HUMAN STRENGTH

Willpower-smart living

Simple habits to protect your energy and support the choices that matter most. (Inspired by the research of Roy F. Baumeister & John Tierny,)

> At its core, willpower is not an endless force to summon at will, but a finite strength, gradually worn down by the decisions and demands of daily life. The goal is not to strive harder, but to create a rhythm that respects your energy and places what matters most within reach.

At the start of the day

Begin with a task that holds meaning for you: before the noise of the world intrudes. Establish your priorities before opening your phone or checking messages. Nourish your body; low blood sugar quietly undermines clarity and resolve. Where possible, reduce decision fatigue by preparing clothes, meals, or your schedule in advance, conserving focus for what truly requires it.

During the day

Devote your clearest attention to work that calls for emotional presence or mental clarity. Group similar tasks to reduce the cost of constant switching. Notice the impulse to seek comfort in distraction, and pause to consider what is genuinely needed in that moment. If a decision feels clouded or hurried, let it wait. Some choices are best made when the mind is rested and steady.

At the end of the day

Let your evening become a conscious descent, not a collapse. Prepare quietly for the next day—lay out what you need, clear a small space, note a single intention. Reflect with self-respect. The measure is not perfection, but presence. Rest is not a reward for productivity; it is the foundation of discernment and strength.

A final note

Enduring willpower does not arise from relentless effort, but from rhythms that protect and replenish your energy. Self-control is less about heroic resistance and more about shaping your environment and habits to support your deepest commitments.

> *In singlehood, you find the freedom to align with your essence. This season can become a powerful transformation, if you let it unfold without rushing."*
>
> — JACE STERLING

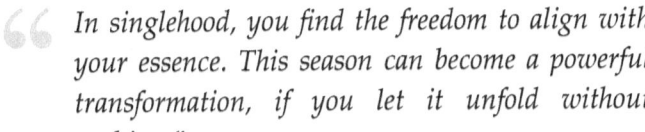

An important distinction

What is the difference between Willpower, discipline and endurance?

Understanding the distinction between willpower, discipline, and endurance is essential for anyone seeking real, sustainable change.

Willpower is a limited, short-term resource. It helps you resist temptation or make tough choices in the moment, but it can quickly become depleted, especially after a day filled with decisions or challenges.

> Discipline is less about constant self-control and more about creating systems, habits, and environments that reduce your reliance on willpower.
> When you intentionally design your routines and surroundings to support your goals, staying on track becomes more natural and less effortful.

Endurance, also known as perseverance or grit, is the capacity to keep going over the long term, particularly when things become difficult. True endurance is sustained not by brute force, but by the supportive habits and systems you've built over time.

In short: Willpower gets you started, discipline keeps you consistent, and endurance helps you finish.

By building supportive habits and environments, you make lasting change not only possible, but far more achievable. Consider where you can shift from relying on sheer will to designing a life that supports your growth.

> *People with strong self-control spend less time resisting desires than others. Developing good habits and routines enhances self-control."*
>
> — ROY F. BAUMEISTER & JOHN TIERNY, WILLPOWER: REDISCOVERING THE GREATEST HUMAN STRENGTH

19

FIRING YOUR STORYTELLER

The stories we tell about past relationships shape not only our memories but also our future possibilities. In the aftermath of pain, it is tempting to craft narratives that protect us from deeper truths, stories where we cast ourselves as victims of others' limitations or failures. Over time, these stories can harden into automatic scripts, repeated so often to ourselves and others that biased recollections begin to feel like objective truth.

We all have a storyteller in our mind, a narrator that stitches experiences into meaning. But unless we remain curious and vigilant, that narrator can trap us in old interpretations, blinding us to the assumptions and habitual filters that keep us stuck.

Yet these protective stories, while comforting, often obscure opportunities for profound self-discovery.

Consider the difference between *"I gave everything and got nothing in return"* and *"What was I seeking through my giving?"* The first story ends in bitterness. The second opens a door to understanding our own patterns and needs.

Growth lies in the questions we often resist asking: Why did we choose what felt familiar over what felt right? What fears drove our need to prove our worth? What boundaries did we fail to honour within ourselves before others crossed them?

This is not about self-blame, but about reclaiming our power to reshape our patterns. Every relationship, especially those that end, offers a mirror not just of another's limitations, but of our own opportunities for growth. When we loosen our attachment to old truths and observe our inner storyteller with curiosity, we create the freedom to move through life with greater fluidity, wisdom, and self-respect.

Soul note

Interrupt your justifications

Reflect

It's easy to become loyal to the story that protects us. After pain or loss, we often cling to narratives that justify our feelings, our decisions, or our sense of self. Sometimes those stories are true, but not the whole truth.

"I gave everything and got nothing back", might feel accurate, but it can also stop us from asking, *"What was I trying to earn through my giving?"*

Growth begins when we start questioning the versions of the story that ask for sympathy instead of clarity. What truth have you been avoiding because it disrupts your role in the script?

Try this

Think of a familiar story you've told yourself or others about a past relationship. Notice where it places blame, where it seeks understanding, and where it might be protecting you from seeing your own patterns. Now, try rewriting the final paragraph of that story. You don't need to change the facts. Just explore a new perspective that gives you back your power.

Mantra

I am the author of my future story.

Self-soothing dialogue

I don't need to get it all perfect. But I do owe myself honesty. It's okay that some of my old stories helped me feel safe or understood. They weren't wrong, they were just incomplete. I can be kind to the parts of me that needed protection and still choose to look closer. Even if the truth is uncomfortable, I can face it because freedom lives on the other side of honesty.

Grounding practice

Sit quietly and place one hand on your heart, the other on your belly. Say aloud, "This is where I begin again." Let your breath settle. On your next inhale, silently ask, "What truth have I been afraid to say?" There's no need to force an answer. Just listen.

Shared truth

> *Victimhood is such a compelling story, but it's not a healing story. It's a story that keeps you stuck."*
>
> — GENEEN ROTH

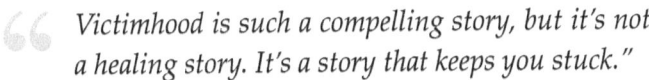

> *The way you choose to think and speak about yourself (to yourself and others), is a choice!*
>
> *"You may have spent your whole life talking about yourself in a negative way, but that doesn't mean you have to continue that path."*
>
> — MIYA YAMANOUCHI

Interrupting our familiar love stories

The stories we repeat about love often protect us from discomfort, but they can also keep us stuck. Use this page to gently question familiar narratives and explore what deeper patterns or fears might lie beneath. Greater self-awareness opens the door to more conscious choices, deeper connections, and lasting growth.

Familiar story - What this might be hiding

- *"I always give too much in relationships."* - Over-giving to feel worthy, manage anxiety, or avoid addressing imbalances.

- *"Nobody appreciates everything I do."* - Seeking validation or avoiding the work of setting clear boundaries.

- *"I'm just unlucky in love."* - Avoiding responsibility for choices, repeating unconscious patterns.

- *"All the good ones are taken."* - Shielding against vulnerability or disappointment.

- *"My ex ruined my life."* - Reluctance to examine personal agency in relationship dynamics.

- *"I'll never find someone who understands me."* - Fearing true intimacy or being fully seen. Avoiding responsibility for connections made.

- *"Everyone else finds love easily."* - Comparing to others, to avoid engaging in genuine self-discovery and growth.

- *"I'm better off alone. Relationships are too painful."* - Using past hurts as armour against future vulnerability.

- *"No one will ever love me like they did."* - Clinging to familiar pain to avoid risking new possibilities.

- *"I don't chase, I attract."* - Justifying passivity; avoiding active engagement or vulnerability.

- *"If it's meant to be, it will be."* - Abdicating agency; avoiding effort, risk, or honest communication.

- *"The right person will just show up when I'm ready."* - Magical thinking; reluctance to take relational risks or clarify desires.

- *"I'm waiting for someone to choose me."* - Reinforcing patterns of passivity and unworthiness.

- *"Love should be effortless."* - Avoiding the necessary work of building and sustaining healthy relationships.

- ***"I don't want to settle, so I'll just wait."*** - Using high standards to shield against vulnerability or intimacy.

- ***"The universe will send me my soulmate."*** - Magical thinking; avoiding personal responsibility for relational outcomes.

- ***"If they really want me, they'll pursue me."*** - Belief that initiative equals desperation; fear of rejection; lack of self-advocacy.

Reflective prompts:

- Which of these familiar stories have you told yourself?
- What might become possible if you replaced waiting or blaming with conscious, courageous action, even small steps, toward the connection and life you desire?
- Try journaling about one familiar story. What emotions or memories arise when you question what might be beneath it?

> *We must be willing to let go of the life we've planned, so as to have the life that is waiting for us."*
>
> — JOSEPH CAMPBELL

20

DETHRONE YOUR INNER-CRITIC

The inner critic is not just a voice: it is a throne we build in our own minds, crowning doubt and fear as rulers over our lives. Without realising it, we often grant this voice far more authority than it deserves, treating its harshest assessments as truth rather than the remnants of old wounds.

> Dethroning the inner critic is not about silencing every doubt, but about reclaiming the seat of judgment for ourselves, choosing curiosity and self-respect over automatic self-condemnation.

Between every thought and its meaning lies a moment of choice. Yet certain inner narratives become so familiar, they masquerade as absolute truths. Often born in moments of past hurt or disappointment, these stories quietly shape how we see ourselves and what we believe is possible.

Our inner dialogue is not background noise; it is the architect of our experience. Each time we silently accept "I'm not enough" or "This is all I can expect," we are not just describing life; we are defining its boundaries. These quiet conclusions shape every decision that follows, steering whether we reach for more or quietly settle for less.

Such internal narratives often become self-fulfilling. We accept treatment that mirrors our lowest expectations, unconsciously seeking evidence to confirm the inner critic's familiar refrain. This is not about forced positivity. It is about recognising that the beliefs we allow to sit on the throne shape the limits of what we invite into our lives.

Breaking free from negative self-talk requires more than surface encouragement.

> It demands the courage to face the inner critic with curiosity instead of compliance. These voices are not inborn truths; they are patterns we picked up along the way. Seeing them as learned, not natural, makes it possible to question and release them.

Every time we consciously challenge a limiting belief, we engage in a quiet act of rebellion against inherited doubt. With vigilance and compassion, we can begin to loosen the critic's grip and reclaim the authorship of how we see ourselves and what we believe is possible.

This process is neither quick nor effortless. Yet in the space between thought and meaning, possibility waits: patient, steady, and ready for us to choose a different story.

Soul note

Becoming your most loyal advocate

Reflect

The inner critic often echoes old wounds, speaking in voices that once held authority. Over time, those echoes can start to sound like facts. Notice whose voice you're hearing, and ask yourself what might shift if you began to advocate for yourself instead.

Try this

Write down three things your inner critic says. For each one, write a compassionate truth that reflects who you are now, not who you were when those doubts first took root.

Example:

- Critic: "You always mess this up."
- Truth: "I'm learning, and I deserve patience."
- Let your truth sound like something you'd say to someone you love.

Mantra

I am the advocate my younger self needed.

Self-soothing dialogue

Sometimes it feels like my inner voice isn't on my side. I know it means well, trying to protect me from rejection or disappointment, but it doesn't always see the full picture. That voice is shaped by fear, not truth. I'm learning to listen without letting it take over. I don't need to silence it, just remind it that I'm taking the lead. I've survived my hardest days. I'm here now, steady and present, becoming the advocate I needed then and still deserve today.

Grounding practice

Gently place your hands over your ears. Let this physical gesture mark a boundary between yourself and the critic's voice. Breathe slowly. On your next exhale, say quietly, "I decide what gets to stay." When you're ready, move one hand to your heart. Acknowledge the part of you that deserves peace.

Shared truth

When we get lost in the trance of unworthiness, we live in a story of separation—from others, from the world, and from ourselves."

— TARA BRACH

Negative thoughts: RAIN

A gentle path through negative thoughts (Mindfulness teacher Tara Brach popularised the RAIN framework.)

Understanding RAIN

Difficult thoughts, like passing storms, do not define us. RAIN offers a compassionate approach to navigating moments of emotional turbulence and self-criticism with awareness and kindness.

- **R**ecognise what's happening in your mind. Notice when critical thoughts arise without trying to change or suppress them.
- **A**llow the experience to be there. Give yourself permission to feel what you feel, without rushing to fix, minimise, or judge it.
- **I**nvestigate with gentle curiosity. Explore what lies beneath these thoughts with kind, open attention, not analysis or blame.
- **N**urture with understanding. Offer yourself the compassion you would extend to a dear friend facing the same inner struggles.

This practice does not eliminate difficult thoughts, but it transforms your relationship with them. Instead of being swept away by self-criticism, you learn to hold space for your experience, remaining steady and centred as the storms pass through.

Negative thinking

 You can turn every ugly and damaging drama into a genuine blessing by seeing it differently.

"No one is suffering on purpose. We learn to give up the pleasure we feel in self- righteously blaming others.

"Healing happens when we see things differently. The question is: do you want suffering or peace? It's that simple."

— DONNA GODDARD, WALDMEER

 The primary cause of unhappiness is never the situation but your thoughts about it."

"Some changes look negative on the surface but you will soon realise that space is being created in your life for something new to emerge."

— ECKHART TOLLE, A NEW EARTH: AWAKENING TO YOUR LIFE'S PURPOSE

21

NO MORE WAITING

Gratitude opens our eyes to the abundance already flowing through our lives. When we release the mindset of waiting, waiting for the perfect partner, the perfect moment, the perfect life, each day reveals its hidden treasures: the freedom to follow our inner guidance, the space to nurture meaningful connections, and the opportunity to explore life's infinite possibilities.

This sacred time allows us to be fully present with those we cherish. We can spend unhurried mornings with our children, create precious memories, or simply be there when family needs our full attention. Evenings might find us laughing with friends, teaching a pet new tricks, or enjoying an unhurried connection.

> Without the constant negotiation of partnership,
> we discover an extraordinary gift: time to
> invest in personal growth and creative pursuits.

Whether launching a passion project, studying spiritual teachings, or mastering a new craft, we can dive deep into our interests without compromise or explanation.

What others may see as solitude, we recognise as sacred space to hear our own wisdom, to grow without permission or apology. Gratitude is not about forced positivity. It is about discovering the richness already available in this chapter of life, no more waiting required.

Lived insight

For years, I postponed my dream of going back to university. There was always a reason: money, timing, responsibility. But beneath it all, I quietly feared it might be too late. After my separation, I realised I could no longer wait for perfect conditions or anyone else's permission. I applied anyway. When I received my acceptance letter, I felt seen: proud, uncertain, and quietly determined. For the first time in a long while, I believed it was time for me to have a chance at pursuing a dream that had felt out of reach for so long.

I am still working to make it happen. Writing this book is one way I am investing in the future I want to build. I am not waiting anymore. This is what hope looks like now: quiet, determined, and mine to carry.

Soul note

Practicing gratitude

Reflect

Gratitude is not a performance. It's a quiet act of noticing what sustains you, even when things feel unfinished. Without waiting for perfection, recognise what's already working: moments, comforts, and connections that are easy to overlook when you're focused on what's missing.

Try this

Set a timer for 2, 3, or even 5 minutes. Give yourself space to settle and collect your thoughts. List three ordinary moments from this week that felt steady or nourishing: sunlight through a window, finishing a small task, or hearing laughter. Let it be simple and real. Take longer if you wish. Absorb the warmth of the sun, feel the breeze on your face. Let this be a moment to step away from performance and reconnect with your present self.

Mantra

I let gratitude anchor me in the present. I release the idea that I need to earn rest, joy, or fulfilment. I welcome the life I have today, even if it is still unfolding. I trust that I can find contentment now, without waiting for everything to align. I remind myself that this chapter is enough, and so am I.

Self-soothing dialogue

I'm not on hold. I don't need to wait for everything to be in place before I feel grateful. Even when things feel unfinished, I can still notice what's good today. Gratitude helps me stay grounded in what's real. Today, I close my eyes and choose to breathe. Things will get easier as I adjust and keep moving forward.

Grounding practice

Stand barefoot on a flat surface. Name one thing you're grateful for aloud. Feel the vibration of your voice in your chest and the solidity of the floor beneath you. Repeat twice, letting your words settle you in the now.

Shared truth

 Happiness never comes to those who fail to appreciate what they already have."

— BUDDHA

Celebrating singlehood

> *You are your own best company, and no one knows how to make you happy better than yourself."*
>
> — BELLA DEPAULO

> *Single is an opportunity to live life on your own terms and not apologise for it."*
>
> — MANDY HALE

> *In solitude, we discover our strength and creativity, unclouded by external expectations."*
>
> — RUMI

> *Being single allows you to write your own story, free of interruptions or rewrites."*
>
> — KETURAH KENDRICK

> *Being single isn't a time to look for love; use that time to work on yourself and grow as an individual."*
>
> — AUTHOR UNKNOWN

Going solo

 Living alone helps us pursue sacred modern values—individual freedom, personal control, and self-realisation—whose significance endures from adolescence to our final days.

"It allows us to do what we want, when we want, on our own terms. It liberates us from the constraints of a domestic partner's needs and demands, and permits us to focus on ourselves.

"Today, in our age of digital media and ever expanding social networks, living alone can offer even greater benefits: the time and space for restorative solitude. This means that living alone helps us discover who we are, as well as what gives us meaning and purpose."

— ERIC KLINENBERG, GOING SOLO: THE EXTRAORDINARY RISE AND SURPRISING APPEAL OF LIVING ALONE

22

LETTING THE FUTURE UNFOLD

We often navigate singlehood as if it were a temporary harbour, anxiously scanning the horizon for approaching ships or gazing back at those that have sailed away. Yet in this constant looking elsewhere, we miss the treasures that lie in the depths of now.

Like stirring a perfectly still lake, our restless seeking creates ripples that distort our reflection. Each thought of "When will love arrive?" or "Why did they leave?" disturbs the crystal clarity that emerges only in stillness. The very waters we trouble already hold everything we seek.

> Present moment awareness invites us to sit quietly at the water's edge, allowing our thoughts to settle until we can see clearly again. In that gentle stillness, we discover our completeness was never lost; the waves of our own seeking simply obscured it.`

When we loosen our grip on past and future, we find that true peace isn't about finding the right person or healing old wounds. It is about coming home to the stillness, the harbour we carry within us, where life in all its fullness continuously unfolds. No more waiting; change happens now.

Soul note

The season you didn't know you needed

Reflect

Change doesn't always begin with a grand decision. Sometimes it starts quietly, in the moment you stop scanning the horizon and simply arrive in your own life. You may not always feel ready. That's natural. Change often stirs both curiosity and caution.

You might sense a shift, but not yet see its shape. That doesn't mean you're lost. It means you're evolving. This season may feel unfamiliar, even unnerving, but it holds potential you haven't yet imagined. You're not starting over. You're building forward, carrying the insight, resilience, and quiet wisdom that experience has taught you.

You're not here to chase the next thing or cling to what's gone. You're here to meet what's unfolding, one grounded moment at a time.

Try this

Make one small change to your routine today. It doesn't need to be dramatic. Swap one habit that feels stale for something that brings energy or presence, like a short walk before your morning coffee or a pause before checking your phone. Let it be simple and conscious.

Mantra

I can learn to trust the season I am in.

Self-soothing dialogue

I don't have to rush or retreat. I can meet this moment with care. Even when I don't feel fully ready, I trust that I'm not starting from nothing. My experience counts. I don't need to force change, only allow space for it to unfold. I can grow through this, gently, honestly, and in my own time.

Grounding practice

Stand tall and let your arms hang loosely by your sides. Begin to sway gently from side to side, feeling your weight shift across your feet. Let your breath match your rhythm. You are not stuck. You are in motion, even here.

Shared truth

 The only place where life exists is the present moment. Miss that and you miss everything."

— ECKHART TOLLE

Concept: ichi-go ichi-e

The Japanese concept of ichi-go-ichi-e teaches that every encounter, every moment, is unique and unrepeatable. Rooted in the traditions of the Japanese tea ceremony and Zen philosophy, this practice invites us to approach life with presence, gratitude, and care, recognising that no two experiences can ever truly be repeated in exactly the same way.

> In daily life, ichi-go ichi-e encourages us to be mindful, focusing fully on the present rather than becoming lost in past regrets or future worries. It asks us to show gratitude for the people and experiences we encounter, treating each interaction with the tenderness and reverence of a once-in-a-lifetime event. It invites us to act with intention, honouring even ordinary days as sacred, and to embrace impermanence, understanding that change and endings give each moment its rare, fleeting beauty.

When we live in this spirit, we discover that the richness we seek is already here, in the conversations we hold, the sunsets we witness, the quiet kindnesses we extend and receive. Even the simplest days become extraordinary when we meet them as if for the first, and only, time.

> 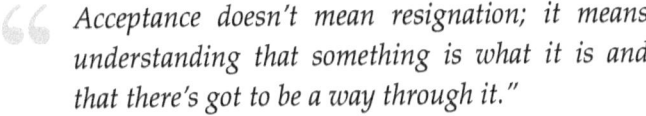 *Acceptance doesn't mean resignation; it means understanding that something is what it is and that there's got to be a way through it."*
>
> — MICHAEL J. FOX

23

THE UNEASE OF MISALIGNMENT

Like radio static interfering with a clear signal, anxiety and depression often arise when we drift from our natural frequency. These emotions are not enemies to defeat but messengers highlighting where we have lost connection with our authentic path.

Each wave of discomfort points to areas where we are maintaining alignments that no longer support our growth. The more tightly we grip outdated patterns, relationships, or beliefs, the greater our distress, signalling what our soul is ready to release.

> Our internal guidance system never stops broadcasting our true direction.

But learned responses such as fear, judgment, and resistance can create interference. This disruption often appears as anxiety when we resist necessary change, and as depression when we deny our natural evolution.

> Healing does not require us to force a new frequency. It invites us to release the resistance that distorts our clarity.

Beneath the noise, our true signal remains: clear, steady, and ready for us to tune in again.

Lived insight

I have come to trust the signals my body sends when something is not right. Misalignment feels like tightness in my chest or a restless prickle under my skin, as if my whole system is on alert. In the past, I often tried to override that discomfort, especially when speaking up meant disappointing someone or walking away from a familiar connection.

But every time I finally honoured what my body was telling me, whether it was leaving a draining job, stepping back from a one-sided relationship, or setting a long-avoided boundary, what followed was unmistakable.

> My breath would ease, my shoulders would drop, and a quiet wave of relief would settle in. That sense of ease became more reliable than logic or approval. It let me know I had chosen well.

Soul note

Learning to trust your inner compass

Reflect

Discomfort is not a flaw but a message. Anxiety can surface when you resist change or try to control outcomes. Depression may linger when you stay too long in situations, beliefs, or relationships that no longer reflect who you are becoming. These feelings can feel isolating, especially when others don't understand or know how to respond. But this unease is a meaningful cue. It is your body, mind, and intuition, all asking for realignment. You don't need to have everything figured out. Start by noticing what feels off, then take small, caring steps to support what has surfaced so your inner dialogue feels seen, heard, and validated.

Try this

Think of a recent moment when you felt unsettled: anxious, disconnected, or low. Pause and ask yourself: What part of me needed something different? What thought, habit, or environment no longer feels right? What gentle shift could bring me into better alignment with what I need now? Let this be a quiet check-in, not a task to solve. No pressure, just curiosity.

Mantra

I am learning to trust my inner compass.

Self-soothing dialogue

I know sometimes I feel unsettled, and that is okay. These emotions are part of a natural shift. For years, I may have ignored my own signals. Now that I am listening, things might feel louder before they soften. That is part of the process. I do not need to fix everything right away. I only need to stay present and pay attention. My job is to create a safe space where I can hear and honour myself. One steady, realigned moment at a time.

Grounding practice

Sit or stand comfortably. Place one hand on your heart and one on your belly. If it feels comfortable, close your eyes. Take a slow breath in. As you exhale, picture a compass gently settling into place. Feel your body supported by the ground beneath you. You are still here, and you are allowed to find your way.

Shared truth

> *The soul always knows what to do to heal itself. The challenge is to silence the mind."*
>
> — CAROLINE MYSS

Anxiety

> *Our anxiety does not come from thinking about the future, but from wanting to control it."*
>
> — KHALIL GIBRAN

> *If you are depressed, you are living in the past. If you are anxious, you are living in the future. If you are at peace, you are living in the present."*
>
> — ANONYMOUS, OFTEN ATTRIBUTED TO LAO TZU

Regulating self

> *The best use of imagination is creativity. The worst use of imagination is anxiety."*
>
> — DEEPAK CHOPRA

> *We humans have lost the wisdom of genuinely resting and relaxing. We worry too much. We don't allow our bodies to heal, and we don't allow our minds and hearts to heal."*
>
> — THICH NHAT HANH

Compression vs. Depression

> *Every single one of you has a natural state, from time to time, called compression... When you are searching for answers you know cannot be found in the outer reflection of the world. You withdraw within where you know all the answers actually lie."*
>
> — DARRYL ANKA (BASHAR)

24

THE PERFECT TIME TO BE SINGLE

Isn't it fascinating how life often gives us exactly what we need, precisely when we need it? Sometimes, being single isn't a gap between relationships; it's life's perfect timing unfolding with remarkable precision. Like a beautifully orchestrated dance, certain chapters call for the unrestrained freedom that only singlehood can provide.

Think of the friend who landed her dream job because she could say yes to every opportunity, or the one who launched her business because her time was her own. That's the power of perfect timing in singlehood. Some of life's most transformative opportunities arrive when we have the freedom to seize them fully.

Even life's challenges seem to call for the clarity of solitude: after heartbreak, when your soul needs rewriting; during grief, when healing demands space; or in post-divorce parenting, when your children need your undivided presence more than you need romantic company. These aren't empty seasons; they are sacred spaces where being single becomes your superpower.

Whether you are advancing your career, healing, raising children, or rediscovering who you are beyond relationships, this single season might be life's way of giving you the uninterrupted time you need to become who you are meant to be.

> Perhaps, in the dance of your life, singlehood is not a pause but the step that carries you closer to your truest rhythm.

Soul note

This season is yours

Reflect

Not every season is meant for partnership. Some arrive to help you reset, heal, and reclaim parts of yourself that were once set aside. This time is not empty or in-between. It is yours, a chapter where your focus can shift inward without apology. Whether you are raising children, rebuilding confidence, or rediscovering joy, singlehood gives you room to move freely, grow deeply, and show up fully for yourself. This season is not a pause. It is part of the dance. It is here to be lived, fully and consciously.

Try this

Name three things you have had the time, energy, or clarity to pursue because you are single right now.

- What have you said yes to?
- What has healed or shifted because you had space to focus on it?
- What are you ready to explore next?
- Let your answers reflect the unique gifts of this season.

Mantra

This season is mine to shape.

Self-soothing dialogue

I am not missing out. I am exactly where I need to be. This time is not a gap. It is a gift. I have space to grow on my own terms, to heal without distraction, and to rediscover what makes me feel whole. I trust that everything meaningful will unfold at the right time. For now, I get to show up for myself in ways I once couldn't. That is not loneliness. It is freedom.

Grounding practice

Open a window or step outside. Feel the air on your skin. Name one thing you appreciate about this chapter of life. Let your breath deepen. Let your body know: this moment belongs to you.

Shared truth

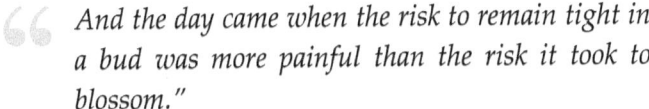 *And the day came when the risk to remain tight in a bud was more painful than the risk it took to blossom."*

— ANAÏS NIN

25

DITCH THE DRAMA

Drama often masquerades as intensity, importance, or justified reaction when it is really an echo of unmet needs seeking expression. Like background music we barely notice, we may not realise how often we tune into frequencies of conflict, comparison, or complaint.

Consider what draws you toward dramatic situations. Is it boredom seeking stimulation? Loneliness reaching for connection through conflict? Or old wounds still searching for validation? These patterns do not make us wrong, they make us human. Yet awareness offers choice, and choice offers freedom.

> The skill is not in avoiding all conflict. Some situations genuinely require our engagement. The art lies in distinguishing necessary confrontation from optional entanglement.

When we catch ourselves being pulled into others' emotional chaos, or creating our own, we can pause and ask, *"Is this enriching my life, or just recycling old stories?"*

True peace is not passive. It is a powerful choice to invest energy in growth rather than grievance. Each time we choose compassion over being right, presence over reaction, we are not just avoiding drama, we are actively dismantling the invisible threads that keep us bound to old patterns.

Like untangling ourselves from a complex web, one mindful choice at a time, we free ourselves from the familiar pull of toxic connections and codependent traps.

Each decision to step back from drama's edge becomes an act of liberation, allowing us to reclaim not just our energy, but our power to write an entirely new story, one where peace is not just the absence of conflict, but the presence of genuine freedom.

Soul note

Not everything needs your energy

Reflect

There comes a time when peace becomes your priority. Not because you are avoiding life, but because you are finally choosing to live it on your terms. Not every spark needs your attention. Not every disagreement deserves your voice. You can choose which moments are worth your energy and which are not yours to carry. Each time you pause before reacting, you create space to notice what is really driving your response. This is not avoidance. It is the beginning of a new kind of power, one that supports your needs and frees your energy for what truly matters. This is the season for quiet power and steady self-respect.

Try this

Identify one situation, conversation, or dynamic you can consciously step back from this week.

Ask yourself:

- *Is this really mine to hold?*
- *What response would actually serve my well-being?*

What can I let go of without explanation?

As you step back, notice if there is a deeper feeling or unmet need beneath the urge to engage. Let this awareness guide your next choice, whether it is setting a boundary, seeking support, or simply letting go. Let this be a pause that nourishes your peace, not a retreat from your strength.

Mantra

I choose peace over chaos. I don't need to match every tone or respond to every spark. I can step back without guilt and still stay true to myself. Calm is not weakness. It is a different kind of strength.

Self-soothing dialogue

Just because there is noise does not mean I need to join it. I am allowed to protect my space. I do not need to absorb every emotion or meet every tone. It is okay to step back. I can keep my energy for what matters. When things feel stirred up around me, I can ground myself in calm. I am not missing out by staying centred. I am showing up for myself in the best way I know how.

Grounding practice

Sit or stand somewhere quiet. Close your eyes if that feels safe. Imagine a gentle rain falling around you. Feel the tension on your shoulders, jaw, and chest softening with each drop. Let this imagined rain rinse away whatever is not yours to hold. Let your breath return to you. This calm is your strength.

Shared truth

> *You do not have to attend every argument you're invited to."*
>
> — UNKNOWN

Understanding drama triggers

When life feels beyond our control, we often seek power in unlikely places. That heated response to a social media post, the surge of road rage, or the pull of office gossip rarely stems from the triggering event itself. More often, these reactions are attempts to reclaim control when we feel powerless in more significant areas of our lives.

Notice how a minor traffic slight can escalate into disproportionate anger, or how a stranger's comment online might trigger hours of defensiveness. These moments of overreaction often mask deeper feelings of vulnerability or frustration elsewhere.

While social media and workplace dynamics can offer connection and creativity, they can also become easy outlets for displaced emotions. Each space where we feel less vulnerable can become a stage for acting out unresolved tensions.

True empowerment lies in recognising these patterns. When we catch ourselves reacting strongly, we can pause and ask, "What area of my life feels out-of-control right now?"

This awareness helps us address root causes rather than perpetuating cycles of drama and reactivity.

> *Between stimulus and response there is a space. In that space is our power to choose our response."*
>
> — VIKTOR E. FRANKL

Ten paths to drama-free living

Drama-free living is not about avoiding challenges, but about meeting each moment with clarity, boundaries, and self-respect. These ten paths offer daily touchstones for cultivating peace, emotional freedom, and intentional living.

1. **Honour Your Boundaries** : Define your limits clearly and defend them calmly.
2. **Curate Your Circle** : Nurture relationships that elevate rather than drain.
3. **Practice Neutral Presence** : Observe without absorbing others' conflicts.
4. **Master the Pause** : Create space between trigger and response.
5. **Engage Mindfully Online** : Choose conscious connection over reactive scrolling.
6. **Embrace Selective Involvement** : Prioritize your peace over others' expectations.
7. **Release the Need to Know** : Let gossip flow past without catching you.
8. **Know Your Triggers** : Cultivate self-awareness as a shield against drama.
9. **Choose Your Battles** : Not every situation deserves your energy.
10. **Cultivate Inner Stability** : Build your peace as the foundation for all else.

Peace is not found in avoiding life, but in meeting each moment with presence, wisdom, and self-respect.

The cost of being 'right'

Think about the last heated discussion where you felt absolutely certain of your position. Recall that familiar surge of frustration when someone would not see your point of view. How often did those moments of certainty and conversational battle actually lead to meaningful change or deeper understanding?

The need to be right often disguises itself as defending the truth, yet beneath it lies a deeper belief: that our perspective is the only one that matters. This mindset turns conversations into battlegrounds where understanding becomes impossible.

We have all experienced both sides of this dynamic: the frustration of being dismissed and the fleeting satisfaction of winning an argument. Yet victory in these moments often comes at the cost of trust, respect, and genuine connection. Each time we prioritise being right over understanding, we reinforce walls between ourselves and others.

When we impose our truth, we sacrifice connection for hollow victory. What might change if we approached disagreements with genuine curiosity?

What becomes possible when we release the need to convince and instead seek to understand?

 People almost never change without first feeling understood."

— DOUGLAS STONE

> *The biggest communication problem is we do not listen to understand. We listen to reply."*
>
> — STEPHEN R. COVEY

> *Settle in the present moment. An unsettled mind either is worrying about the future or traveling into the past. And rejecting, judging about an event that happened into your past."*
>
> — SHI HENG YI, TEDXVITOSHA TALK, 5 HINDRANCES TO SELF-MASTERY

> The single most important thing you can do is to shift your internal stance from "I understand," to "Help me understand." Everything else follows from that.
>
> (Or better yet, shift from "I already know" to "Help me understand.")"
>
> — DOUGLAS STONE, DIFFICULT CONVERSATIONS: HOW TO DISCUSS WHAT MATTERS MOST

26

CAGED BIRDS CAN'T FLY

Compassionate detachment emerges when we recognise that true support honours another's capacity to find their own solutions. Often, this wisdom arrives only after we have exhausted ourselves, pouring energy into rescuing others from challenges they must ultimately face alone.

> To care deeply does not mean protecting others so completely that they lose the chance to strengthen themselves.

Sometimes, without realising it, we create cages for the people we love, taking on responsibilities that are not ours to carry, assuming we must manage or fix parts of their lives. Over time, this misplaced care can quietly erode confidence, autonomy, and self-sufficiency.

While the heart behind it may be tender, controlling, or overprotecting, others can entangle us in patterns of dependency, where growth is stifled rather than nurtured.

In relationships, these patterns often spill into codependency, a dynamic where genuine connection is replaced by rescue, caretaking, or control. True compassion invites a different path.

To care with wisdom is to trust that each person possesses an inner strength that can only emerge when given space to grow. By stepping back from the impulse to intervene, we create the conditions for genuine transformation, both for ourselves and for those we love.

> Letting go of the belief that others need our constant intervention is not indifference; it is a more sustainable, respectful way to care. This shift allows us to stay connected without becoming entangled in dynamics that drain our energy or inhibit another's self-trust.

True compassion means believing in the resilience of others. It is the quiet conviction that our role is not to carry another's burdens, but to trust in their ability to rise. In offering support without becoming their source of strength, we honour the dignity of their journey.

This trust must also extend inward. When we recognise our own capacity to navigate life's challenges, we release the expectation that someone else must rescue or complete us. Self-trust becomes the foundation for authentic interdependence, where relationships enhance our strength rather than define it.

Freedom, for ourselves and for others, begins the moment we stop managing, fixing, or rescuing, and instead witness the unfolding of growth in its own time. **Only then do caged birds remember they were meant to fly.**

Lived insight

My marriage was built on love, but also on a subtle misalignment. I became a motivator and rescuer, believing that if I poured in enough care and hope, we could both rise. Instead, my support became a cage of overprotection and silent expectation, burdening me with responsibilities that were never truly mine.

I see now that love is not about making someone else fly, or shaping their path to match my vision. Letting go was not abandonment. It was an act of respect for both of us.

> Singlehood has taught me to release what was never mine, and to keep lifting myself in ways that feel true.

Soul note

Trust life's detours

Reflect

Compassionate detachment is not indifference. It is the quiet wisdom of trusting that others are capable of finding their own way. When you step back from rescuing or fixing, you create space for genuine growth, both for yourself and for those you care about. This is not abandoning support, but respecting boundaries and trusting others' resilience. Sometimes, the most loving act is to witness, not to intervene.

Try this

Write about a time when life didn't go to plan: perhaps when you stepped back from a relationship, an obligation, or a role you thought you had to play. What wisdom revealed itself in that detour? What did you learn about your own strength or about trusting others to find theirs?

Mantra

I honour the path, even when it turns unexpectedly.

Self-soothing dialogue

It's okay to pause. I don't have to solve everything. Life has its own rhythm, and so do I. Sometimes, stepping back is the most loving choice I can make. I trust that others are capable and that my role is to support, not to carry.

Grounding practice

Stand with feet planted firmly. Stretch your arms out wide. Inhale deeply. As you exhale, turn your palms outward, gently pushing your hands forward, as if offering space. Say aloud or silently: "I release what's not mine to carry."

Shared truth

When you expect another to succeed without the benefit of your help, you will see them as their Source sees them. When you believe another needs your help, and you attempt to shore up their weakness with your strength, you help them not."

— ABRAHAM, ESTHER HICKS

Dependency definitions

Understanding enmeshment, codependency, and releasing responsibility for other adults.

Enmeshment and codependency blur healthy boundaries, making it hard to separate your feelings and responsibilities from those of others. Recognising these patterns is a vital step toward reclaiming your autonomy and allowing others to do the same.

Enmeshment

- Involves unclear emotional boundaries, leading to:

- Difficulty setting limits
- Absorbing others' emotions
- Guilt when asserting independence
- Neglecting your own needs to maintain harmony

Codependency

Is when your sense of worth depends on caring for or managing another, often seen as:

- Chronic people-pleasing
- Difficulty saying no
- Taking responsibility for others' happiness
- Feeling unworthy if not needed

Relinquishing control

Wanting to help is natural, but feeling responsible for another adult's emotions or choices signals unhealthy patterns.

Over-managing can:

- Undermine their growth
- Drain your energy
- Create imbalance and resentment
- True compassion trusts others to handle their challenges. Letting go of responsibility for their well-being respects both you and them.

Moving toward healthy boundaries

Healthy boundaries allow you to care without over-carrying. They support connection without self-sacrifice.

- Notice where you feel overly responsible
- Practice saying no or stepping back
- Support by listening, not rescuing
- Remember: everyone is responsible for their own happiness

Reflective prompt

Where do you feel compelled to "fix" another adult's feelings or choices? What might it feel like to trust both them and yourself enough to step back?

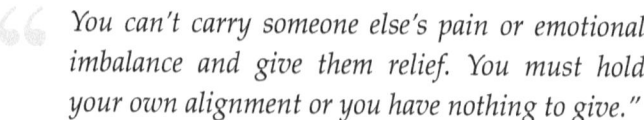

> *You can't carry someone else's pain or emotional imbalance and give them relief. You must hold your own alignment or you have nothing to give."*
>
> — ABRAHAM, ESTHER HICKS

27

SOLITUDE REQUIRES COURAGE

Solitude is not a sign of failure. It is an act of courage, a quiet decision to stay present with yourself, even when the instinct is to run. That pit in your stomach when walking into an empty house, the urge to fill silence with noise, the reflex to reach for your phone, these are natural responses to profound change, not personal flaws.

For those who have lost partners, everyday moments can feel hollow with absence. Parents sharing custody experience sharp cycles of fullness and emptiness. Even those who choose singlehood encounter unexpected waves of loneliness when connection is not immediately at hand.

Beneath resistance to solitude often lie deeper fears: Will this last forever? Am I missing out on life? Who am I without others to reflect me back to myself?

Rather than rushing to escape these feelings, solitude invites us to stay, to meet discomfort with patience, not judgment. Each moment of unease becomes a quiet invitation to build trust in our own company.

> The goal is not to erase loneliness, but to develop resilience, knowing that, like all emotions, it will ebb and flow.

Solitude, when met with courage, becomes a crucible for self-trust. In learning to stand alone, we discover the unshakable strength that was always ours.

Soul note

Finding comfort in solitude

Reflect

Solitude is not a punishment or a sign of failure. It is a space where truth softens into presence. The hardest part is often the beginning, the moment you enter a quiet room and feel the weight of absence. But over time, the silence stops shouting. What once felt empty begins to feel still. This is not about enjoying every quiet moment, but learning to stay with yourself without fleeing. When you do, your presence becomes a steady hand to hold. With patience, this courage allows your inner voice to emerge with greater clarity, a quiet reminder that you are never truly alone with yourself.

Try this

Choose one moment today to be alone with intention, even just ten minutes. Put your phone away, turn off background noise, and notice what arises. Notice if you can stay, just a little longer than feels comfortable.

Mantra

I am brave enough to be with myself.

Self-soothing dialogue

It's okay to feel uncomfortable in the quiet. Solitude is not emptiness; it is an act of courage. I can stay here with myself, even when I don't have answers. This feeling will pass, and I will still be here, steady, breathing, enough.

Grounding practice

Sit or lie down with one hand on your heart. Close your eyes. Inhale slowly. As you exhale, gently say: "I am here." Repeat until your breath softens.

Shared truth

 Sometimes you need to sit lonely on the floor in a quiet room in order to hear your own voice and not let it drown in the noise of others."

— CHARLOTTE ERIKSSON

7 Steps to navigate the fear of being alone

> With gratitude to Tony Robbins for these insights (Source: "Fear About Ending Up Alone," 2024, Tony Robbins Blog).

Solitude can be daunting, but it also offers a profound opportunity for growth. Drawing on Tony Robbins' practical wisdom, these seven steps invite you to reframe the fear of being alone and embrace singlehood with confidence:

- Focus on yourself
- Understand your fear
- Question your blueprint
- Fulfill your top human need
- Let go of the past
- Broaden your connections
- Uphold your standards

These principles encourage a shift from anxiety to self-assurance, reminding us that the journey toward comfort in solitude is both courageous and transformative.

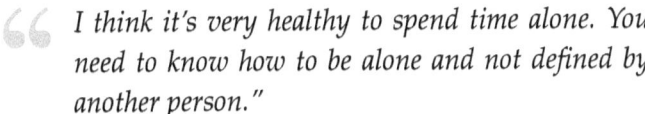 *I think it's very healthy to spend time alone. You need to know how to be alone and not defined by another person."*

— OSCAR WILDE

28
UNTANGLING CODEPENDENCIES

Codependency infiltrates relationships quietly, often disguised as partnership or compromise. Small concessions and convenient role divisions can slowly erode autonomy until we no longer recognise how much of ourselves we have surrendered. What begins as "sharing the load" can harden into patterns of dependency that dim our capabilities and confidence.

The realisation often comes sharply when we find ourselves alone. The gap between who we once were and who we have become reveals itself in countless daily challenges. For single parents, this awakening often means restructuring life entirely around children's needs, sometimes carrying far more than their share.

Overwhelm and resentment are natural responses to these imbalances. Yet embracing full responsibility for our lives, including the hard parts, becomes the path to genuine strength. This is not about denying unfairness. It is about recognising that accepting responsibility for our healing is ultimately empowering.

> Breaking codependent patterns is messy work.
> Each uncomfortable moment is an essential act
> of untangling, a necessary step toward
> independence.

Trust that your commitment to self-reliance will serve you, even on the hardest days. Your struggle is not failure. It is the courage to reclaim your freedom and move toward true interdependence, where strength is shared, not surrendered.

What interdependence really means

Interdependence is not about doing life alone. It means having the capacity to stand on your own feet while still welcoming connection, not out of need, but from a place of strength. It is the balance between autonomy and mutual support. When we are grounded in our own wholeness, we no longer seek completion in others. We seek connection.

> Interdependence allows us to share life without
> losing ourselves.

Lived insight

For much of my life, I believed it was my job to carry what others could or would not. I stepped in, smoothed over, filled the gaps at home, at work, in friendships. I mistook usefulness for love and over-functioning for care. But the more I managed, the less others had to, and I slowly lost sight of where their responsibility ended and mine began.

Letting go of that pattern was uncomfortable. My identity had been built on being reliable and needed. Singlehood exposed how much of that was survival, not choice. I've had to relearn the difference between generosity and self-abandonment. Now, when guilt or resentment rises, I pause and ask: is this truly mine to carry? Love is not performance. Showing up whole means allowing others to do the same.

Soul note

Making interdependence your new bare minimum

Reflect

Letting go of codependent patterns can feel like losing part of your identity. The over-functioning, the quiet resentment, the sense that if you don't hold everything together it will all fall apart, these habits run deep. But your strength was never meant to carry everything alone.

Interdependence is not a luxury. It is your new bare minimum, a way of relating where strength is shared, not surrendered. It means you can stand on your own and still welcome support and love, knowing your worth is not diminished by asking or receiving.

> Untangling these patterns takes time. It requires learning how to say, "This is no longer mine to hold," and trusting that letting go creates space for your own wholeness to return.

Try this

Name one thing you can do for yourself today, without help. Complete the task slowly and with presence. Let it be a quiet act of self-trust.

Mantra

I am enough. No one else needs to complete me. I can share life without surrendering myself. I let connection flow from my wholeness, not my need.

Self-soothing dialogue

It's okay if I leaned on others more than I needed to. That doesn't make me weak or broken. It just makes me human. In close relationships, it is easy to slip into habits of over-relying on someone else. I see that now with more clarity, and I can forgive myself for it.

Today, I get to build new skills, ones that help me feel steady on my own. Even if I choose partnership again, I want it to be grounded in connection, not dependency. I don't need to be rescued, and I don't need to disappear into someone else. I am learning to meet my own needs first. When I love again, it will be from a place of balance, not searching for a rescuer, but standing beside someone who chooses to walk with me.

Grounding practice

Find a knotted necklace, string, or cord. Gently begin to untangle it, one loop at a time. Let this be a mirror of your healing. Be patient, steady, and willing to undo old patterns thread by thread.

Shared truth

Interdependence is the balance between autonomy and connection. When we are grounded in our own wholeness, we no longer seek completion in others. We seek connection. It is a conscious choice to share life with others from a place of strength, respect, and mutual support."

— JACE STERLING

> *True love is not about dependency. It is about two strong individuals choosing to walk side by side."*
>
> — BRENÉ BROWN (PARAPHRASED)

> *The formula is simple: In any given situation, detach and ask, 'What do I need to do to take care of myself?"*
>
> — MELODY BEATTIE, CODEPENDENT NO MORE

> *We rescue people from their responsibilities. We take care of people's responsibilities for them. Later we get mad at them for what we've done. Then we feel used and sorry for ourselves. That is the pattern, the triangle."*
>
> — MELODY BEATTIE

29

TAKE UP SPACE LIKE YOU MEAN IT

Your perspective matters because no one else has lived your story or seen the world through your eyes. Self-validation means protecting that truth and honouring the irreplaceable gift of your authentic voice.

Taking up space begins with trusting your needs and honouring them without apology, simply because you feel them. Let your choices flow from inner wisdom, not from external approval. Your dreams belong to you, not to the limitations or expectations of others.

There is nothing rebellious about claiming the space you were born to inhabit. It is not selfish to speak with your full voice or to meet your own needs, even when others would prefer you quiet, agreeable, or easy to manage.

If you have ever felt pressure to shrink, to avoid upsetting others, to seem less intense, or to stay in alignment with people you care about, you are not alone.

> Sometimes we are asked to play small because our growth reminds others of the ways they have stayed stuck. But shrinking is not love. It is self-abandonment. You no longer owe anyone the comfort of your silence.

You might not always get it right. You may overcorrect as you begin to protect your space and find your voice. That is part of the process. It does not make you unkind. It makes you new. Not everyone will understand your growth. You do not need their approval, nor do you have to carry their discomfort.

> Your expansion does not need to be loud. You do not need to declare what you are building or warn those waiting to dismiss you.

Let it unfold quietly, strategically, and in your own time. It is okay if your growth surprises people, even you.

As you honour your truth, you begin to set clearer boundaries. You grow more discerning about whose voices you allow in, and over time, attract connections that celebrate rather than suppress your authentic expression. Not everyone has earned the right to shape your path, and that is more than okay.

Each time you stand in your truth, you make space for others to do the same. The world does not need you smaller or quieter. It needs you whole, luminous, and unapologetically yourself.

> You are meant to take up space.

Soul note

We shrink for no one

Reflect

Reclaiming your space is not about volume or bravado. It is the quiet, steady decision to remain visible, even when it feels easier to fade. Your presence matters not for what you produce, solve, or soften, but simply because you are here. Whole. Worthy. Enough.

Try this

Choose a space where you feel safe. Stand with your feet firmly grounded, shoulders open, and chin level. For one full minute, focus only on the sensation of being here. Notice your breath, your stance, the room around you. Let yourself feel seen, even if only by yourself. You do not need to explain or justify your presence.

Mantra

I take up space without apology.

Self-soothing dialogue

It's natural to feel small sometimes, especially when you are learning to protect your boundaries and trust your voice. That awkwardness is not failure. It's part of the expansion. Some people may be unsettled by your growth, but their discomfort is not your responsibility. You do not have to shrink to be safe, and you do not owe anyone the comfort of your silence. You can belong to yourself first and still choose connection from that place.

Grounding practice

Hold a soft object such as a scarf, cushion, or folded blanket against your chest. Stand with your feet hip-width apart and inhale gently.

As you exhale, imagine an energy field extending just beyond your body, giving you space to move, breathe, and exist as you are. With each breath, picture it widening just enough to hold you with ease. This is not about walls; it is about permission. Repeat quietly: I am here. I am whole. My space is mine to claim.

Shared truth

> *Your presence is not a disruption. It is a reminder that the world is richer when you show up fully."*
>
> — JACE STERLING

> *Discover why you're important, then refuse to settle for anyone who doesn't completely agree."*
>
> — FISHER AMELIE

When you start giving yourself the validation you've been craving, the need for validation from others begins to fade."

— JACE STERLING

A note to my child

To my dearest daughter,

You are not just strong; you are compassionate, brave, and kind beyond your years. Life has tested you in ways that could have hardened you, but instead, you have chosen laughter, empathy, and a defiant kind of hope that refuses to be dimmed.

Your humour, your fierce heart, and your refusal to be like everyone else are not accidents. They are choices you make every day, and they are your light.

I hope you will always remember that the courage to take up space is not only about standing out when it feels easy, but about staying true to yourself when love, belonging, or acceptance seem to demand that you shrink. You are already everything you need to be.

Never let anyone convince you that you must become smaller to be loved.

*Please don't ever forget that being your mom will always be the greatest gift of my life.
You are forever loved, exactly as you are.*

*All my love - always,
Mom.*

30

MORE THREADS, LESS TENSION

Single life weaves new threads into our social fabric, revolutionising how we approach friendship and family. Without the pressure to merge identities with a romantic partner, we remain fully ourselves across different circles, expressing unique aspects of our personality with friends and family members.

> By creating more threads in our social fabric, we reduce the tension that comes from relying on one connection to meet all of our emotional needs.

Notice the freedom of attending a family gathering solo, fully present for deep conversations with siblings or playful moments with nieces and nephews. Or showing up for spontaneous coffee dates, sharing unfiltered thoughts without negotiating anyone else's schedule. This freedom allows genuine connections to deepen and thrive, threading together moments of joy and shared understanding.

> Single people often build strong, diverse relationships because they don't rely on one person to meet all their emotional needs. Each friendship offers different forms of support and connection.

Your academic friend challenges your thinking. Your adventurous friend pushes your boundaries. Your childhood friend holds your history. Family members can become closer confidants when interactions are unfiltered by a partner's presence.

These varied threads create a rich, resilient tapestry where you are free to be multifaceted, not merged into a coupled identity.

> You are not just someone's better half. You are a whole person, woven into a vibrant community of connection, strength, and joy, threads that hold each other up and create the fabric of your rich life.

Soul note

Build your single era support network

Reflect

Support networks in single life often don't look the way we expected. They shift over time, and that's not a problem to solve but something to accept. Who do you turn to when you need honesty, laughter, calm, or comfort? Are there people you feel close to but often overlook? Are there relationships that feel one-sided or no longer fit? Pay attention to what feels nourishing and what feels absent. You have the freedom to shape your network with care.

Try this

Reach out to someone you would like to reconnect with or include more intentionally in your life. It might be a colleague you admire, a friend you miss, or a relative you trust. Keep it simple and manageable: like a quick call, a walk, or sharing something that made you think of them. You do not need to force depth. Just begin.

Mantra

I am free to build the network that supports who I am choosing to become.

Self-soothing dialogue

I give myself permission to build a support system that reflects who I am and what matters to me. My connections don't need to follow a script to be meaningful. Some people bring insight, others bring peace, joy, or honesty. I do not need to depend on one person for everything. It is okay to let go of relationships that feel heavy or unbalanced. There is room in my life for connection that feels mutual, energising, and real.

Grounding practice

Write down the names of three people who help you feel grounded, seen, or supported. They can come from any part of your life. Next to each name, note one way that they have positively impacted your well-being. Let this remind you that support shows up in different forms, and that your circle does not have to look conventional to be strong.

Shared truth

> *Each friend represents a world in us, a world possibly not born until they arrive."*
>
> — ANAÏS NIN

> *Friendship is a love story... Different from romantic or filial love, it's its own unique love story. Making friends is the first free choice relationship we have as kids. Our friends provide community and continuity in an ever- changing world. Our lifelong friends are our witnesses.*

> "They accompany us through the trials and tribulations of lovers that come and go, job changes, family rifts, births, deaths, and recoveries. And we are a witness for them, commiserating or celebrating together over morning coffee or late-night phone calls."
>
> — ESTHER PEREL, LETTERS FROM ESTHER #27: FRIENDSHIP, ACCESSED DECEMBER 8, 2024.

> *Time doesn't heal. It's what you do with the time. Healing is possible when we choose to take responsibility, when we choose to take risks, and finally, when we choose to release the wound, to let go of the past or the grief."*
>
> — DR. EDITH EGER

31

SINGLE LOOKS GOOD ON YOU

Single life offers an unparalleled opportunity to prioritise your well-being without compromise. Research shows singles often maintain better physical health habits, exercising more, sleeping soundly, and making food choices aligned with their own needs.

The benefits extend beyond the physical. Without the emotional labour of maintaining a relationship, singles often experience less stress and greater mental clarity. **You are free to process feelings at your own pace, set boundaries that protect your energy, and create routines that support your psychological health.**

This autonomy ripples through every aspect of life. From scheduling check-ups without coordinating calendars to nurturing friendships that boost longevity, singles have unique advantages in building sustainable wellness practices.

Most significantly, singlehood allows you to

develop robust self-care skills that serve you for life. Instead of outsourcing emotional well-being, you learn to meet your own needs, physically, emotionally, and socially.

This self-sufficiency becomes a foundation for lasting health, whether you remain single or choose partnership.

Thriving in your singlehood may unsettle others, especially those who feel threatened by your autonomy or well-being. Jealousy or discomfort from others is not a reflection of your worth, but of their own struggles. Seek out those who celebrate your independence and respect your journey. Trust that your happiness does not diminish anyone else. You deserve to take up space and live freely.

Lived insight

I've always been sensitive to other people's energy, so after my separation, living alone wasn't just peaceful. It was healing. Without the constant presence of someone else's moods, I could finally hear my own. My body softened, my sleep deepened, and my breath no longer caught in my chest. With no one to manage or tiptoe around, my nervous system began to settle in ways it never had. Singlehood didn't just look good on me. It gave me my health back, and with it, a life that finally felt like mine.

Soul note

Your body, your life, your choice

Reflect

Single life brings a kind of clarity that is often overlooked. Without adjusting your habits to fit someone else's, you can listen to your own rhythms and care for your body in ways that feel genuinely good. This is not selfish; it is self-stewardship. Consider what it means to feel well in your own skin. What would it look like to prioritise your health and energy without needing anyone's permission?

Try this

Choose one small act today that supports your well-being. You might skip a social commitment that drains you, take a walk at your own pace, stretch before bed, or prepare a meal that suits only you. Keep it simple and make it yours.

Mantra

I am free to honour what makes me feel strong, clear, and well. I care for my body and mind on my own terms. This life is mine to nurture and protect.

Self-soothing dialogue

I am not here to perform wellness for anyone else. My choices can be quiet, personal, and true to what I need.

When I feel tired, it is okay to rest. Sometimes that means taking the day off and gently disconnecting from old habits that once kept me too busy or too tired to care for myself. I am allowed to find balance in my body without debate, explanation, or permission. Whether I move, rest, heal, or simply pause, how I care for myself is mine to decide. My well-being is valid, even when it looks different from what others expect.

Grounding practice

Put on something that makes you feel comfortable and confident. It could be a favourite shirt, a meaningful ring, or a scent you love. Notice how it feels against your skin and let it remind you: this is your body, your life, your choice.

Shared truth

Caring for myself is not self-indulgence, it is self-preservation."

— AUDRE LORDE

Single individuals often report higher levels of personal growth and self-care practices than their married counterparts."

— DR. JENNY TAITZ

> *Single people tend to be more fit because they don't have someone else's schedule, preferences, or eating habits to deal with."*
>
> — BELLA DEPAULO, SINGLED OUT: HOW SINGLES ARE STEREOTYPED, STIGMATIZED, AND IGNORED, AND STILL LIVE HAPPILY EVER AFTER, 2006.

> *I didn't realise that being single was the gift my soul had been craving. These days, I feel stronger, healthier, and more myself than I've been in a long time."*
>
> — JACE STERLING

> *The solitude of single life can actually enhance mental wellbeing when approached with the right mindset."*
>
> — MANDY HALE

The Guardian – Survey

> *"No, being single doesn't make me miserable"*
>
> *53% of unpartnered GenZ and 59% of single millennials said they preferred being single to being in a relationship."*
>
> — SURVEY STATFROM A 2024 SURVEY BY THE SURVEY CENTER ON AMERICAN LIFE:

32

DORMANT DREAMS

When a partnership ends, whether by choice or circumstance, you are invited to rebuild and reimagine your life's direction. Like a tree losing its familiar support, you're called to grow new roots, deeper and stronger than before.

> This isn't about filling the space left by another's absence. It's about rediscovering the quiet whispers of purpose that may have faded during your coupled years.

What dreams did you set aside? Which parts of yourself went unexplored while tending to partnership?

Think of this chapter as awakening from a long sleep. As your eyes adjust to the light, you notice desires and aspirations that transcend relationship status. Perhaps it's a creative project, a career pivot, or personal growth you postponed. These are not distractions from being single. They are portals to your authentic path.

The beauty of this reconnection lies in its power to heal old regrets.

> Each step toward your neglected dreams is an act of self-reclamation. You are not just filling time until love returns; you are choosing to love yourself enough to pursue what truly matters to you.

By reconnecting to the dreams you've set aside, you embrace the power to create your future, independent of past limitations.

Soul note

Your chance to build a life you can love

Reflect

Some dreams arrive before we are ready to carry them. Others get reshaped by life's demands. Right now, you have a rare opportunity: to build forward with full awareness. There may be distance between where you are and where you want to be, but that space is not a reason to hold back. It is an invitation to grow into the version of you who can hold what you are creating. What would it look like to honour your future with action, even if you do not have every detail worked out yet?

Try this

Choose one small step that aligns with the life you want to create. It might be something bold, like enrolling in a course or pitching an idea. Or it might be something quieter, like setting a boundary or waking up early to reclaim time. Do not wait until you feel ready. Begin, and readiness will meet you.

Mantra

I am building toward the life I want, one decision at a time.

Self-soothing dialogue

I do not need certainty to move forward. I trust myself to meet what comes, even if it is unfamiliar. Every brave choice I make today strengthens the future I am shaping. I can stretch into discomfort without abandoning myself. I have the right to build a life that feels meaningful, on my terms and in my own time.

Grounding practice

Close your eyes and take a slow, steady breath. Picture a seed nestled in the earth-quiet, full of potential. Imagine warmth and moisture reaching it, and see the seed begin to swell and crack open. Visualise a tiny shoot pushing upward, breaking through the soil, reaching for the light.

Let yourself feel the quiet hope and energy of this new growth. Remind yourself: your dreams can awaken and take root, no matter how long they've been dormant

Shared truth

> 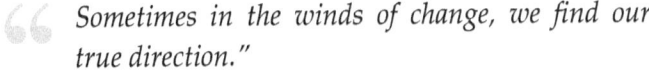 *Sometimes in the winds of change, we find our true direction."*
>
> — UNKNOWN

33

YOUR LIFE, YOUR BLUEPRINT

Creating your life's blueprint requires more than setting goals. It's about designing a life grounded in your values: defining the principles that guide your choices when no one else is setting your direction.

Values differ from morality.

While morality often comes from external rules and expectations, values are rooted in personal truth. They show up in what energises you, what you defend instinctively, and what you prioritise when no one is watching.

> Building your vision isn't about checking off achievements. It's about understanding how your core values, whether innovation, justice, learning, or connection, translate into daily decisions.

Every choice, from how you spend your mornings to which opportunities you pursue, shapes the reality you're creating.

This process requires radical honesty about what truly matters to you versus what you've inherited from others' expectations. Your blueprint gains strength when it springs from authentic values, not from external pressures or predefined success.

Designing your life is an ongoing process of self-discovery and intentional choice. Let your values guide you and build a life that is uniquely yours.

Soul note

You have a lot of living to do

Reflect

Your values aren't just abstract ideas. They are the living pulse behind how you shape your days. Whether you're starting fresh or recalibrating your path, this moment invites you to reconnect with the life you still want to live. You don't need to justify why something matters to you. You are allowed to keep dreaming, keep planning, and keep choosing. Your time is not over. You have a lot of living to do.

Try this

Sketch a blueprint for your ideal day. Focus not on productivity, but on alignment. What time do you wake up? What kinds of activities, people, or choices appear? What values are reflected in those choices? Then choose one small part of that day to bring to life tomorrow.

Mantra

I have more life to live, and I get to decide what it looks like. I am learning to trust my values to guide each choice I make. This is my time to build what matters to me.

Self-soothing dialogue

There is no expiration date on the life I want to create. I am not late. I am not behind. I can carry old dreams forward and welcome new ones. Even if others can't see it yet, I trust that my life is still unfolding in a way that matters. I don't need certainty to begin. I only need to stay connected to what feels real and meaningful. I can honour who I am and who I am becoming at the same time.

Grounding practice

Draw a simple symbol that represents one of your core values. Choose something personal and true. It can be abstract or literal. As you draw, connect to that value not just as a word, but as a quiet truth that lives within you.

Shared truth

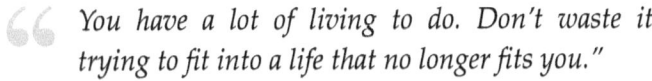 *You have a lot of living to do. Don't waste it trying to fit into a life that no longer fits you."*

— UNKNOWN

34

YOUR HOME, YOUR HAVEN

Sharing life with someone brings beautiful compromises: mutual choices that reflect love, connection, and shared experience. Those carefully chosen furnishings, colours, and mementos are more than objects; they are reminders of shared growth and meaning.

There's deep value in these symbols of partnership and the art of blending lives harmoniously.

> Singlehood offers a different kind of opportunity: the chance to consciously curate your environment around your authentic self. This isn't about dismissing the past; it's about granting yourself permission to evolve beyond it.

Keep the photographs that warm your heart and the gifts that still resonate, while releasing anything that dims your natural inclinations.

Your space now holds the potential to reflect your unfiltered preferences. Ask yourself: What would you choose if no one else's comfort zone influenced your decisions? Every intentional choice becomes a declaration, a physical affirmation of reclaiming and expressing the self you are becoming.

When I first redesigned my living space, it became a personal revolution. My dramatic lounge room, with its immersive black walls, tan leather sofas, and that one defiant bright pink cushion, whispers to me daily "I am home, and this is a safe space to be fully me."

Your home is your haven. Let it be more than a place to live. Let it become a daily reminder that you are free to create a space, and a life, that fully expresses who you are.

Lived insight

After my separation, I bought new furniture and painted the walls, hoping a fresh start would follow. But while the space looked pleasant and practical, it lacked lustre. The artist in me had vanished under the weight of marriage, motherhood, and survival. I hadn't realised how much I needed creative, calming spaces to regulate my nervous system and reconnect with myself. For the first time in years, I didn't have to negotiate colour palettes or apologise for my style. I painted the lounge black, hung striking Iris Van Herpen fashion design artworks, and filled the space with bold, expressive details.

My home continues to evolve. When I walk through the door, I don't just feel at home. I feel seen, validated, and celebrated by myself.

Soul note

Your home is your sacred space

Reflect

It is easy to disappear in shared spaces. To make small compromises, soften your preferences, or tuck parts of yourself away to keep the peace. Over time, a home can become a place where your presence feels muted. This chapter of your life offers something different. You are free to create a space that reflects who you are becoming. This is not about erasing the past. It is about making room for your full self. Your home is allowed to feel personal, grounding, and entirely yours.

Try this

Choose one small corner of your home and begin shaping it into a space that reflects you. It might be a reading nook, a windowsill, your bedside table, or a favourite chair. Experiment with scent, lighting, colour, softness, or sound. Select one object that brings you comfort, peace, or lightness.

If you feel ready to be bolder, take bigger steps. Paint a wall. Redecorate a whole room. If possible, redesign your home gradually and let it evolve alongside you. Revisit each space in stages so it reflects not only who you were, but who you are becoming. This is not a one-time project. It is a living process of self-discovery and self-expression.

> Give yourself permission to release anything that carries heaviness or unwanted memories. You do not need to keep what no longer serves you. Let this process be intuitive.

Wander through an op shop. Scroll through Marketplace. Explore slowly. You are not shopping for approval. You are seeking what makes your body breathe easier and your mind feel more at peace.

If your space feels chaotic or neglected, start gently. Each time you enter a room, return one item to its place. Just one. Spend ten minutes a day tending to your space. It does not need to be perfect. It only needs to become more aligned with how you want to feel. If you live with ADHD or executive dysfunction, use a simple planning app or voice memo to set one small step each day. This is not about achieving a polished outcome. It is a shift in how you honour yourself.

Mantra

My home creates space for me to be myself.

Self-soothing dialogue

I am allowed to create a home that honours who I am and what I need. I can prioritise comfort, softness, and beauty, not for others, but for myself. My sensory needs matter. Whether I need soft lighting, warm textures, airflow, quiet, or gentle sound, I am allowed to choose what supports my well-being. Every detail I add is a quiet affirmation: I deserve to feel safe here. I belong here.

Grounding practice

Sit in the space you have created or reshaped. Notice the colours, textures, sounds, and objects around you. Touch one item you chose with care. Feel how it holds a piece of your story. Let this space become part of your rhythm. Return to it often to breathe, stretch, reflect, or rest. Let it remind you that you are not lost in this space. You are home.

Shared Truth

> *Your home should tell the story of who you are, and be a collection of what you love."*
>
> — NATE BERKUS

> *The ache for home lives in all of us—the safe place where we can go as we are and not be questioned."*

— MAYA ANGELOU

> *Your home should be a reflection of who you've become, not a reflection of what you've left behind."*

— SUZY KASSEM

35

FUTURE YOU SAYS THANKS

Close your eyes for a moment and imagine your future self, stronger, freer, standing a little taller because of the choices you're making now. They smile at you with genuine gratitude and say, "Thank you for not giving up when it would have been easier to stand still."

> The path to proactive personal growth isn't always clear or comfortable, especially when you're juggling single parenthood, mounting bills, and limited support. Some days, simply keeping everything afloat feels like achievement enough. Yet this is exactly when investing in your future becomes most critical. Not because it's easy, but because staying still is the riskiest option of all.

Reality check: Learning new skills while exhausted from work and parenting isn't glamorous. Studying part-time when you can barely keep your eyes open, starting a side hustle between school pickups, or writing that book in stolen moments is a grinding journey.

> Married parents may understand the tiredness, but rarely the weight of doing it alone.

The pressure to secure your financial future, manage care, and handle all the parenting logistics may sit squarely on your shoulders, with no backup plan or partner's income, time, or support to rely on.

This isn't about overnight success stories. It's about small, persistent steps toward greater independence, even when progress feels painfully slow. Maybe it's one online course this year, a certification next year, or gradually building freelance skills while maintaining your day job. Or it might be finally carving out time for exercise, starting therapy, creating art, or nurturing a practice that restores your wellbeing.

> Every small investment in yourself matters, even if results aren't immediately visible.

Don't wait for perfect conditions to start. Begin where you are, with what you have. Take that free online course. Start that small side business. Apply for that promotion. Write that book. Not every venture will succeed, but each attempt teaches valuable lessons and opens unexpected doors.

Your future self will thank you for the grit, the faith, and the quiet courage you showed, especially on the days when it felt almost impossible.

Soul note

Deliberate. Uncomfortable. Worth It.

Reflect

Change that matters is rarely comfortable, and it is never handed to you. The world will not pause to reward your effort, nor will anyone else make your future their priority. If you want a different life, you have to create it: deliberately, persistently, and often without applause. This is not about waiting for the right moment, the right recognition, or someone else to notice your potential. It is about putting your head down and doing the work, especially when it feels inconvenient or unseen. Growth means investing in yourself, not just when it is easy, but precisely when it is hard, when you are tired, when others doubt you, when the comfort of routine tempts you to coast.

Whether it is upskilling for career leverage, building a creative outlet, or pushing into a new fitness or service challenge, the act of finishing what you start is not about fun or external validation. It is about refusing to let yourself down.

> No one else will fight for your expansion. You are the only one who can define the terms of your future.

If you need to study in the car while your child is at music, do it. If you need to wake at 4am, do it. The discipline to keep going, especially when it would be easier to stand still, is the quietest, most powerful form of self-respect.

Try this

Take a clear-eyed look at one area of your life where you have settled for comfort or routine, where you sense you could grow but have not challenged yourself in a while. This might be professional, creative, physical, or even about service to others. Ask yourself: Where have I stopped expanding? What skill, capacity, or experience, if developed, would give me more freedom or leverage two or three years from now?

Write a list of possibilities without worrying about how you would afford them, where you would do them, or what others might think. Let yourself explore widely: learning a language, building a side business, deepening financial literacy, mentoring someone for free, or taking on a physical challenge. You do not need to act on everything. The point is to notice what is missing, the presence of which would make a significant difference in your life. Clarity comes from seeing what you have outgrown and what is quietly waiting to be claimed.

Mantra

I do not wait for a better time. I build my future by refusing to give up on myself.

Self-soothing dialogue

This is not meant to be easy. I do not need to enjoy discomfort, but I am willing to face it. I am not doing this for applause or recognition. I am doing it because I want to be someone I can count on, especially when things get tough, when no one else is watching, and when the outcome is uncertain. Each time I show up, I prove to myself that I am worth the effort.

Grounding practice

Sit upright, feet firmly on the floor. Place your hand over your heart and feel its steady weight. Breathe in slowly, and as you exhale, say aloud: "I keep my word to myself. I finish what I start. I am building something that lasts."

If you like, pick up a small object, a smooth stone, a pen, or your keys and hold it in your palm for a minute. Let its weight remind you of your own presence and commitment. This is not about intensity. It is about showing up, quietly and consistently, for yourself.

Shared truth

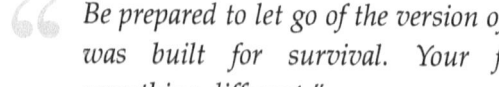
Be prepared to let go of the version of yourself that was built for survival. Your future wants something different."

— ANONYMOUS

> *The secret of change is to focus all of your energy not on fighting the old, but on building the new."*
>
> — SOCRATES

> *You cannot change your destination overnight, but you can change your direction overnight."*
>
> — JIM ROHN, THE FIVE MAJOR PIECES TO THE LIFE PUZZLE (1991)

> *If you don't design your own life plan, chances are you'll fall into someone else's plan. And guess what they have planned for you? Not much."*
>
> — JIM ROHN, 7 STRATEGIES FOR WEALTH & HAPPINESS: POWER IDEAS FROM AMERICA'S FOREMOST BUSINESS PHILOSOPHER (1985)

36

WHAT BECOMING LOOKS LIKE

That first sip of morning coffee from your favourite mug, or slipping on a lucky bracelet before a big meeting, these aren't just habits. They are declarations of self-expression. Personal rituals and meaningful tokens serve as anchors of identity, especially potent during seasons of solo living.

> Each small act of care becomes a quiet rebellion, a statement that your space, your energy, and your wellbeing matter.

That flower delivery isn't about decoration, it's a celebration of your worth. The aromatherapy diffuser isn't just about soothing scents, it is a daily reminder you have the right to create an environment that nurtures your spirit. Even choosing bold shoes or enjoying an exquisite meal becomes an act of joyful self-validation.

These rituals aren't about filling emptiness or distraction. They are conscious choices, small acts of sovereignty that shape your life's direction. Whether it's a morning meditation, a curated playlist, or a cherished piece of jewellery that reminds you of your strength, each ritual is a living expression of your authentic self.

What matters isn't the ritual's size, extravagance, or perfection, but how deeply it resonates with your journey. These daily practices become touchstones of identity, reminders that you're not just passing time. You are actively crafting a life that reflects, honours, and quietly rebels for who you truly are.

Lived insight

> This book wasn't written from a place of perfect arrival. It was written in the midst of new and unplanned challenges. I've stumbled, started over, doubted myself, and learned to hold grace alongside grit. Growth has not been tidy. It has been uneven, awkward, and unexpectedly beautiful and restorative.

I've stopped chasing flawless progress and instead learned to return to myself, over and over. Each time I honour what feels true, it becomes harder to abandon myself. That quiet commitment may not be loud or fast, but it is the kind of progress I trust now. It is what I am most proud of.

Soul note

I choose me

Reflect

Becoming often begins in quiet moments: a song you play on repeat, a scent that makes you exhale, a small choice that feels undeniably yours. These aren't just habits. They are acts of allegiance. They say, I'm still here. I still matter. Choosing yourself isn't about escaping responsibility. It's about making space for your own needs and longings. This is not self-indulgence. This is self-loyalty.

Try this

Begin one daily ritual that feels like an honest expression of you. It could be a short playlist to start your day, a scented candle before bed, or a moment to stretch before anyone else needs you. Let it be simple, personal, and easy to return to, even when life feels full.

Mantra

I choose me, every day. It's okay to make mistakes along the way. I am learning to show up for who I am and who I am becoming.

Self-soothing dialogue

It's normal to hesitate when I put myself first. Some days it feels natural. Other days I worry it's selfish or there's no time. But I remind myself: I'm worth showing up for, even when I'm tired or unsure. Lighting a candle, spraying perfume, making tea, or putting on earrings just because they lift me is not indulgence. It's a reminder. It tells my inner world that I matter, even if no one else sees it. This is how I build trust with myself, one small act of care at a time.

Grounding practice

Choose a sensory anchor that brings comfort. It could be something fragrant like essential oil, perfume, or a candle, or something textured like a smooth stone or soft fabric. Take a few slow breaths as you hold or sense it. As you inhale, quietly say, "This moment is mine." As you exhale, "I choose me." Let this small ritual mark your quiet return to self.

Shared truth

> *The privilege of a lifetime is to become who you truly are."*
>
> — CARL JUNG

> *Self-care is not self-indulgence, it is self-preservation."*
>
> — AUDRE LORDE

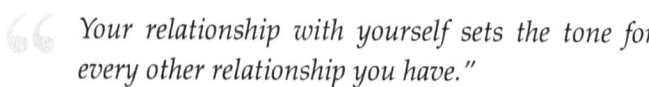
Your relationship with yourself sets the tone for every other relationship you have."

— ROBERT HOLDEN

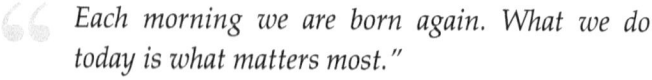
Each morning we are born again. What we do today is what matters most."

— BUDDHA

37

ALLOWING INNER GUIDANCE

Singlehood offers a sacred space to hear yourself more clearly, yet trusting your inner wisdom still means navigating between genuine intuition and seductive distractions. Intuition is not a mood or a fantasy. It is the steady practice of receiving messages from self, subconscious, and source, and daring to act on them.

> **Two common traps distort intuition: spiritual bypassing and toxic positivity.**

Spiritual bypassing often hides in destiny-driven beliefs. The "twin flame" story suggests that chaos and conflict are proof of a destined bond. This convinces many to remain in destructive dynamics, mistaking pain for meaning. That is bypassing, using a mystical label to avoid facing difficult truths and necessary endings.

Toxic positivity appears in slogans like "I don't chase, I attract." At first, it sounds empowering. But taken literally, it implies that life will hand you everything without effort or discernment. Optimism matters, but when positivity denies discomfort or discourages action, it becomes toxic. It dulls the very signals that are meant to guide you forward.

Neither bypassing nor toxic positivity brings wisdom. Both hold you in illusions of progress and transformation by presenting themselves as enlightened concepts, while quietly encouraging you to step back from accountability and the boundaries that shape a life you can truly claim as your own.

> True intuition needs aligned action to create meaningful impact. It grounds you in honesty and points toward intentional steps.

Practices such as meditation, movement, or time in nature open the space where messages can surface. It is also a warning system, showing you when something is not for you, when a dynamic has soured, or when a relationship has quietly run its course.

Reliable intuition asks you to notice where you may have minimised red flags or rationalised behaviour. It requires distinguishing authentic soul connections from the addictive rush of limerence.

Surround yourself with friends who balance optimism with realism, and choose personal growth content that expands your worldview. Diverse perspectives from science, art, or philosophy sharpen your ability to tell wisdom from wishful thinking.

Intuition may arrive as a feeling of peace or unease in your body, a synchronous conversation, an insightful journal entry, a random thought that wakes you, or a dream that lingers. But unless you act on it, the message fades into wasted insight, leaving only the illusion of progress.

Spirituality is not about collecting profound-sounding ideas. It is the work of translating guidance into lived choices. Genuine intuition strengthens because it moves you. It clarifies, steadies, and dares you to honour what you already know and to act on it.

Trust that life will keep shifting. With patience and practice, you can grow more agile, finding less stress in change because you are living with closer alignment and gently course-correcting along the way. Being intuitive is not something you need to learn. It is already within you. The task is simply to unlearn what gets in the way of hearing your inner voice and recognising its guidance.

Soul note

Listening within

Reflect

In the quiet of singlehood, your intuition has room to breathe. True guidance does not arrive in a rush or a wave of longing. It shows up as calm clarity, a steady presence that does not compete with urgency or fantasy. With so much noise from spiritual soundbites to romantic mythologies, it is easy to confuse emotional intensity with intuitive insight. But real knowing tends to feel grounding, not gripping.

Notice which moments leave you clear, and which leave you stirred but scattered. Your inner compass is already working. You are simply learning how to read it.

Try this

Recall a recent gut feeling, one you followed or ignored.

Write about it:

- What did it feel like in your body?
- Was it quiet or insistent?
- Did it bring peace or urgency?

This is not about judging your choice. It is about learning the signals that guide you best.

Mantra

My intuition is wise. I am learning to trust its quiet messages instead of chasing noise. Right now, I can act on the guidance already given to me.

Self-soothing dialogue

I do not need loud signs or perfect certainty. My inner wisdom often whispers. Even if I have misunderstood it before, I can learn. Each time I listen honestly, I grow more attuned. This is not about getting it right. It is about being real with myself.

Grounding practice

Place your hands over your belly. Breathe slowly. Let your awareness settle where your hands rest. On each inhale, say quietly, "I am listening." On each exhale, "I am steady." Let the rhythm remind you that your inner compass works best when you are calm.

Shared truth

> *Your inner knowing is your only true compass."*
>
> — JOY PAGE

> *If you want to awaken all of humanity, awaken all of yourself. If you want to eliminate the suffering in the world, eliminate all that is dark and negative in yourself.*
>
> *"Truly, the greatest gift you have to give is that of your own self-transformation."*
>
> — LAO TZU

> *Every emotion that you feel is, without exception, communication from your Inner Being letting you*

know, in the moment, the appropriateness of whatever you are thinking, speaking, or acting.

"In other words, as you think a thought that is not in vibrational harmony with your overall intent, your Inner Being will offer you negative emotion. As you do or say something that is not in vibrational harmony with who-you-are and what you want, your Inner Being will offer you negative emotion.

"And, in like manner, when you are speaking, thinking, or acting in the direction of that which is in harmony with your intentions, your Inner Being will offer you positive emotion."

— ABRAHAM, ESTHER HICKS, THE LAW OF ATTRACTION: THE BASICS OF THE TEACHINGS OF ABRAHAM

38

MAKING SPACE FOR WHAT MATTERS

Singlehood offers something rare: uninterrupted space to observe your real needs without apology. No one else's preferences are shaping the noise level, the lighting, the pace of your day, or the expectations placed on your body. For many, this kind of space is unfamiliar. But it is also deeply instructive.

Some of us grew up in homes that were volatile, chaotic, or emotionally demanding. Others spent years in relationships where compromise meant shrinking or adapting to the comfort of others. When the environment finally quiets, you begin to hear yourself more clearly. These truths surface gradually, revealed only in the absence of disruption.

> For some, silence is the foundation of safety. For others, soft textures, dim lights, or predictable routines are not mere preferences. They are what make life liveable. You might realise you

think more clearly when alone, or that what you once saw as a flaw was simply the lifelong drain of overstimulation, a mismatch with your environment. This is not self-indulgence. It is self-stewardship.

Tending to your unseen needs means recognising what helps you feel calm, focused, and well, and making space for those conditions to exist, even if no one else understands them. Whether you are curating your environment, managing your health, or learning how your energy ebbs and flows, the act is the same: making space for what sustains you.

Once the world quiets, your true needs emerge. Not as demands, but as invitations to design a life that fits. The challenge, and the gift, is to listen and respond.

This chapter is not about self-care in the trendy sense. It is about becoming fluent in your own needs, designing a life that respects them, and recognising that doing so is a form of clarity and power. Whether you are aging solo, navigating illness or neurodivergence, or simply claiming the peace you never had, you are allowed to live in sync with yourself.

> You are not too much. You are not too sensitive.
> You are learning how to belong to yourself.

Consider what environments, rituals, or rhythms help you feel most at home in yourself. Let these become non-negotiable, not as explanations, but as declarations of who you are becoming. This is your quiet revolution.

Soul note

What sustains you?

Reflect

Recall a recent day spent alone. What small changes in lighting, sound, routine, or the way you arranged your space made things feel steadier or easier? Notice what worked, even if it was subtle. Let this be quiet noticing, not self-judgment.

Try this

Draw a simple comfort map of your space. Note three details, sensory, practical, or emotional, that help you feel more at ease, and one that tends to unsettle or drain you. Choose one small adjustment to try this week. Maybe it's lowering the volume, moving a chair, or keeping a familiar object nearby. Pay attention to how this shift affects your mood or focus. There's no need to get it perfect.

Mantra

I can shape my space to support what works for me.

Self-soothing dialogue

It's okay to need quiet, rhythm, or comfort. I don't have to explain or defend what helps me function well. Small changes matter. What supports me is real, even if no one else notices.

Grounding practice

Settle into a comfortable position, either seated or lying down. Let your body rest in whatever way feels supportive. Choose one object in your space, such as a mug, a book, a pillow, or a patch of light. Rest your gaze on it or gently hold it in your hands. Notice its texture, temperature, or shape. Take a slow breath in, and as you exhale, allow your focus to stay with that one detail. If your thoughts drift, return to it. This is a moment of presence, not performance.

Shared truth

> *Sometimes the smallest shift in your mindset and your surroundings can change your whole day."*
>
> — UNKNOWN

> *Give yourself the freedom to explore, to learn, to simply be in your own time, at your own pace. You deserve and need the time and the space and*

the opportunity to freely, openly, safely, wholeheartedly discover who you are and who you're supposed to be, free from fear, free from accusation, free from expectation."

— CHLOÉ HAYDEN, DIFFERENT, NOT LESS: A NEURODIVERGENT'S GUIDE TO EMBRACING YOUR TRUE SELF.

Rest and self-care are so important. When you take time to replenish your spirit, it allows you to serve others from the overflow. You cannot serve from an empty vessel."

— ELEANOR BROWN

39

LIVE YOUR MESSAGE

Legacy is not just about what we leave behind; it is about how we choose to live now. While others frantically chase relationship milestones, this season of singlehood offers a profound invitation to explore your deeper purpose and unique contribution to the world.

> Consider how many people delay their calling, waiting for the "right time" or the "right relationship" before pursuing what matters most.

Yet your gifts, insights, and potential impact are needed now. Whether it is mentoring others through similar life transitions, creating art that speaks to unspoken truths, or building something that will outlast you, your purpose transcends your relationship status.

This is not about pressure to achieve or prove your worth through accomplishment. It is about recognising that your experiences, even the painful ones, have equipped you with the wisdom that others need. Your divorce story might help another woman find her courage. Your journey through grief could light the way for someone else's healing. Your choice to live authentically single might inspire others to trust their path.

Think beyond traditional definitions of legacy. Your impact might be quiet but profound, like the daughter who shows her mother a different way to be happy, or the friend whose courage to start over gives others permission to change.

> Every time you choose growth over comfort, authenticity over approval, you are not just changing your life; you are expanding what is possible for others.

Soul note

Create a greater purpose

Reflect

Legacy is not a distant milestone. It is shaped every day by how you choose to show up, especially in seasons when others might be waiting for the right circumstances. Your life, as it is now, reflects what matters most to you and quietly opens the door for others to do the same.

Whether your impact is visible or unseen, you are already shaping what it means to live fully, on your own terms.

Try this

Stand in front of a mirror. Speak a truth you've come to hold that reflects who you are or what you believe. It might be a lesson learned, a value held, or a quiet conviction. Let the words settle. This is not about persuasion or performance. It is about witnessing your own voice, as it stands today.

Mantra

My life is my message. I am here to be myself and to allow permission for my truth to show. I only need to live one authentic choice at a time.

Self-soothing dialogue

I do not have to wait to make an impact. I can live my message now, in small, steady ways. I can mentor, create, share, or support. Not to prove my worth, but because my lived experience carries value. Even when no one notices, the way I choose to live shapes what becomes possible for myself and for others.

Grounding practice

Sit or stand comfortably. Take a slow breath and speak your mantra aloud: "My life is my message." Let the words settle in your body as you breathe. Repeat quietly if you wish, or simply allow them to echo inward. This is not about performance. It is about presence.

Shared truth

> *The meaning of life is to find your gift. The purpose of life is to give it away."*
>
> — PABLO PICASSO

> *Don't ask yourself what the world needs. Ask yourself what makes you come alive, and go do that, because what the world needs is people who have come alive."*
>
> — HOWARD THURMAN

> *Most people want to hear or tell a good story. But they don't realise that they can and should be the good story. That requires intentional living. It is the bridge that crosses the gap to a life that matters."*
>
> — JOHN C. MAXWELL, INTENTIONAL LIVING: CHOOSING A LIFE THAT MATTERS

40

EXPAND YOUR WORLD

There comes a point, often after the inward turn and quiet recalibration, when something deeper begins to stir. Not a desire to go back, or a need to fill space, but a quiet sense that there is more of life to meet.

If you have already embraced a dating pause, this is not a repeat. It is an evolution. **A deliberate expansion into new experiences, beyond the boundaries of romance or routine.** Having tended your inner landscape, you now have the freedom to explore the wider world with fresh eyes.

It is easy to settle into comfort zones that once protected you. Familiar streets. Predictable interactions. Spaces where you know exactly who to be. But comfort and fulfilment are not the same. At some point, safety begins to dull your senses instead of steadying them. This chapter invites you to notice where your world has grown too small and to stretch beyond those boundaries. Let your curiosity, not your competence, lead the way. The goal is not mastery. It is presence.

This might look like joining a small group where sharing is encouraged and your voice is welcomed, or finding a space where your usual confidence gives way to listening and learning. For some, it may be taking a class in something you know nothing about, or saying yes to the kind of invitation you would normally decline. Even something as simple as exploring a new neighbourhood on your own can become a meaningful act of expansion.

> Do something unfamiliar. Let yourself be slightly awkward. Be new at something again. This is not about reinvention. It is about reengagement. You are not here to perform or prove. You are here to feel more alive. Let your world get bigger. Let yourself meet it as you are now.

Soul note

Expand your world

Reflect

Life gets small when we stop paying attention. We repeat the same routes, revisit the same conversations, and fill time with predictable patterns. Not because they bring us joy, but because they feel familiar. But comfort is not always connection. And routine is not the same as growth. This chapter of your life invites something new. Not reckless reinvention. Just deliberate expansion. A stretch. A breath of fresh air through a part of you that has gone unused. You do not have to become someone else. You just have to meet more of who you already are.

Try this

Choose one small discomfort this week. Something you would normally scroll past or say no to. It could be visiting a new cafe alone, joining a community event online, or trying something outside your usual rhythm. If you tend to stay quiet, try speaking up. If you are always leading, let someone else guide. This is not about achievement. It is about shaking up the default setting and noticing what part of you stirs awake in the process.

Mantra

I am open to discovery. I let curiosity guide me into new spaces. I am willing to let life get bigger. I trust that I am capable and resilient enough to adapt and grow in the midst of change.

Self-soothing dialogue

Trying something new does not mean I was doing life wrong before. It just means I am still growing. It is okay to feel unsure, to feel awkward, even to wonder what I am doing. I am allowed to stretch without needing to master anything. Curiosity is enough. I do not need a big outcome. I just need to stay open and see what meets me there.

Grounding practice

Taste something new. A spice you have never used, a dish from a culture you are unfamiliar with, or even a childhood snack you have not had in years. As you eat, pause to notice texture, flavour, and feeling. Let the unfamiliar anchor you in presence, not performance.

Shared truth

> *Life begins at the end of your comfort zone."*
>
> — NEALE DONALD WALSCH

> *Do not go where the path may lead, go instead where there is no path and leave a trail."*
>
> — RALPH WALDO EMERSON

> *The journey of self-discovery begins when we become aware of our limitations and start questioning them."*
>
> — ATTRIBUTED TO SHI HENG YI, VIA QUOTESANITY.COM

41

BEYOND YOU: BEING OF SERVICE

Community service opens doors to profound personal evolution, often in unexpected ways. Beyond helping others, you find yourself surrounded by remarkable teachers, fellow volunteers who model the art of giving with grace, authenticity, and clear boundaries.

Observing others in service provides invaluable insights into human nature. Some see giving as a transaction and become frustrated without recognition. Others contribute with joy, unconcerned with acknowledgment. These contrasts illuminate your own motivations, helping you align service with authentic values rather than external validation.

Regular volunteering develops practical wisdom about sustainable giving. You learn to assess your capacity honestly, say no to prevent burnout, and recognise when to step up. This balance comes through direct experience, not theory.

Every role teaches something new. Leading projects builds delegation skills. Working with long-term volunteers shows how to sustain enthusiasm. Even difficult interactions reveal the link between mindset and fulfilment. These lessons deepen your ability to serve and expand your understanding of human connection.

Contribution thrives in both structured and spontaneous forms. Regular volunteering creates impact, but everyday moments offer endless opportunities to extend kindness: buy coffee for a stranger, help a neighbour, mentor online, or simply listen. These small gestures weave a tapestry of connection that enriches our shared human experience.

> Service is both a gift to others and a path of growth for yourself.

Lived insight

During one of my loneliest seasons, living alone in Sydney and recovering from a breakup, I found steadiness in being of service.

> I volunteered for nearly three years, sometimes up to twenty five hours a week, not to escape my pain, but to remember that I still had something to offer.

The work was humbling and grounding. It reminded me that my presence mattered. Healing does not always come from turning inward. Sometimes, meaning returns in the simple act of showing up for others.

I learned that service, when practiced with boundaries and intention, is not about being indispensable or earning approval. It is about reconnecting with your own worth. That insight has stayed with me, even now. Writing this book is a continuation of that same impulse: to give from wholeness, not depletion.

Soul note

Your presence is a gift

Reflect

Service reveals who you are beneath habits of performance. When you give your time, care, or energy without seeking recognition, you begin to understand the deeper reasons why you give and where it costs you. Not every act of generosity comes from wholeness; sometimes, it is a quiet request to be seen. Notice your patterns of giving. What energises you? What leaves you depleted? Sustainable service doesn't ignore these truths; it includes them.

Try this

Choose one small act of service this week. Let it be quiet and unannounced. Pay attention to how it feels in your body and what stories your mind tells about it. Afterwards, ask yourself: Did I feel connected, depleted, inspired, or unnoticed? Let your answers guide how you choose to give moving forward.

Mantra

I offer what is mine to give, without abandoning myself. I give from steadiness, not to prove my worth, but to reflect it. I trust that serving others can expand my perspective in ways that help me grow.

Self-soothing dialogue

I do not need to be everything for everyone. I can offer care without overextending. My presence is enough, even when it is quiet. Even when it goes unseen. I give from steadiness, not to prove my worth, but to reflect it.

Grounding practice

After a simple act of kindness, such as holding a door, sending a check-in message, or offering help, pause. Place your hand on your chest. Breathe in gently. As you exhale, say to yourself, "This was enough." Let the stillness affirm the quiet value of your contribution.

Shared truth

> *The best way to find yourself is to lose yourself in the service of others."*
>
> — MAHATMA GANDHI

> *How wonderful it is that nobody need wait a single moment before starting to improve the world."*
>
> — ANNE FRANK

> *Volunteers do not necessarily have the time; they just have the heart."*
>
> — ELIZABETH ANDREW

I have learned that it is by serving that we learn how to serve.

> When we engaged in the service of our fellowmen, not only do our deeds assist them but we put our own problems in fresher perspective. When we concern ourselves more with others, there is less time to be concerned with ourselves."
>
> — SPENCER W. KIMBALL

No time like the present

> If you want to touch the past, touch a rock. If you want to touch the present, touch a flower. If you want to touch the future, touch a life."
>
> — AUTHOR UNKNOWN

> In Zen they say there are only two things: You sit, and you sweep the garden. And it doesn't matter how big the garden is. As you quiet your mind and listen to your heart, you discover that your spirit will not be satisfied unless you also tend your garden. Pick something you care about. It can be local or global, reducing racism or fighting climate change.

"Educate yourself, make close friends with others who are different from you, join the local school board, volunteer at the hospital, work for a political cause, or help the school plant a garden. Lower your carbon footprint. Add your voice and energy. Plant seeds for a more compassionate future. You can't change it all, but your freedom empowers you to contribute to the world, and your love gives you the way to do so."

— JACK KORNFIELD, NO TIME LIKE THE PRESENT: FINDING FREEDOM, LOVE, AND JOY RIGHT WHERE YOU ARE, 2017.

YOUR NEXT CHAPTER BEGINS

Singlehood, as you have lived it, is not a pause between stories. It is a powerful chapter in its own right, now evolving into something richer. Through seasons of solitude and self-inquiry, you have confronted old beliefs, discovered unexpected strengths, and shaped a life that reflects your deepest values. This is not an ending. It is a conscious renewal.

Reflect on how far you have travelled. You have learned to trust your own wisdom, to set boundaries that honour your truth, and to create meaning on your own terms. You are no longer waiting for completion; you are the creator of your life.

> Remember the quiet victories along the way, when solitude became sacred, when you declined connections that no longer served your growth, or when you chose to pursue a dream once set aside.

Each choice has built the foundation of your self-trust and authenticity.

> As you close these pages, honour the courage it took to invest in your own wholeness.

Whether you moved through these chapters sequentially or let your intuition guide the way, your commitment stands as testament to your resilience and self-respect.

What remains with you now? Perhaps it is the clarity of conscious boundaries, the richness of chosen friendships, or the quiet power of daily rituals. Let the tools you found here accompany you, not dictate your path.

> This book is not meant to gather dust.
> Return to these insights when you seek
> > perspective. Share your discoveries with those walking a similar road.

Growth is not a destination, but an ongoing choice to honour your authentic self.

You are not merely surviving singlehood. You are redefining it. Your life holds meaning and power because you choose, shape, and inhabit it fully.

> This is your time, unapologetically, completely, as you are.

> *If I must erase myself to love you, then we're not writing a love story. We're erasing two souls. Real love adds to who we are; it doesn't subtract from who we're meant to be."*

— JACE STERLING

THE CATALYSTS OF CHANGE

Understanding the Singlehood Trend

Before exploring the catalysts behind the rise of single living, particularly among women, I want to acknowledge the work of Eric Klinenberg.

His book, **Going Solo: The Extraordinary Rise and Surprising Appeal of Living Alone** (2012), offered invaluable clarity as I explored this trend. Klinenberg's research illuminated how women's increasing independence, evolving cultural attitudes, and shifting demographics have transformed living alone from a supposed fallback into a conscious, empowered choice.

His insights mirrored what I have witnessed firsthand: living alone is not a failure, not a pause between stories, but a legitimate and evolving way of living, one that many of us are quietly redefining on our own terms.

See "References for this book" chapter for the full reference list.

1. **Women's Independence:** Increasing economic and social independence of women, driven by higher education and successful careers, has reshaped the perception of marriage from a necessity to a choice. [19]
2. **Post-Divorce Singlehood:** Between 33% and 45% of divorced women in their 40s and 50s choose not to remarry, appreciating singlehood for personal growth, financial independence, and freedom. [20]
3. **Changing Societal Attitudes:** Singlehood is increasingly accepted as a valid lifestyle choice. As Sharon Mbakile states, "Single by choice is no longer a radical concept, but a reality for many." [21]
4. **Baby Boomer Impact:** Rising divorce rates among adults 50+ are linked to Baby Boomers' marital instability, increased life expectancy, and changing societal norms. [4]
5. **Focus on Personal Growth:** Post-divorce singlehood allows women to prioritise self-care, explore new interests, and focus on personal aspirations. [21]

> *The extraordinary rise of solitary living is the biggest social change that we've neglected to identify, let alone examine... After all, living alone serves a purpose: it helps us pursue sacred modern values—individual freedom, personal control and self-realization—that carry us from adolescence to our final days."*
>
> — ERIC KLINENBERG, TIME MAGAZINE

REAL WORLD SINGLE STATISTICS & TRENDS

See "References for this book" chapter for the full reference list.

Demographic and Marital Trends:

- **Single adulthood is rising:** Nearly 4 in 10 adults (**38%**) between the ages of **25** and **54** in the U.S. are single, a rise from **29%** in 1990. [1]
- **Marriage rates are declining:** In 1960, **72%** of American adults were married; by 2020, this figure had dropped to **50%**. [2]
- **People are marrying later in life:** Median age at first marriage in 1960: **20** for women, **23** for men. By 2020: **28** for women, **30** for men. [3]

Divorce Trends:

- **Divorce is rising among older adults:** Divorce rate for adults aged **50** and older doubled between 1990 and 2015. [4]
- **Many marriages end in divorce:** 40–50% of married couples in the U.S. divorce, with higher rates for subsequent marriages. [5]
- **Education helps protect marriages:** Couples with college degrees have a **30%** lower divorce risk than those with only high school education. [6]
- **Money fights increase divorce risk:** Couples arguing about finances weekly are **30%** more likely to divorce than those disagreeing about finances less frequently. [7]
- **Women initiate most divorces:** Women initiate **70%** of divorces among heterosexual couples. [9]
- **Conflict is the leading cause of divorce:** Top reasons for divorce: **58%**—arguing/conflict, **45%** — marrying too young, **38%**; financial problems. [10]
- **Married couples with children have a lower divorce rate:** Couples with children have a 40% lower risk of divorce than childless couples. [8]

Widowhood:

- **Widowhood is increasing:** The number of

widowed individuals in Canada increased from **1.55 million** in 2000 to **2 million** in 2022. [11]
- **Widowhood is common among older women:** More than **40%** of Swedish women are widowed by age **80**, making widowhood the most common civil status in this age group. [23]
- **Widows represent a significant global population:** Globally, widows account for **9.1%** of the female marital age population. [24]
- **Older women are far more likely to be widowed than men:** In 2021, **47.1%** of women aged **80–84** were widowed, compared with **16.6%** of men in the same age group. [25]

Singlehood and Unpartnered Statistics:

- **More adults have never married:** The percentage of adults who have never married rose from **9%** in 1960 to **33%** in 2020. [2]
- **Single-parent households are more common:** In 2020, **23%** of children **under 18** lived with a single parent, up from **9%** in 1960. [12]
- **Men are increasingly unpartnered:** By 2019, **39%** of men were unpartnered compared to **36%** of women. [1]
- **Middle-aged adults are more likely to be single:** Among adults ages **40** to **54**, the unpartnered share increased from **24%** in 1990 to **31%** in 2019. [1]

- **Many prefer singlehood to unhappy marriages:** **64%** of Americans stated they would prefer being single over staying in an unhappy marriage. [13]
- **Most singles are content with their status: 67%** of single adults report being happy with their single status and not being married. [14]
- Living without a partner is increasingly common: The share of U.S. adults living without a spouse or partner climbed from **39%** in 2007 to **42%** in 2017. [15]
- **Young adults are more likely to be single:** Roughly **61%** of adults younger than **35** were living without a spouse or partner in 2017, up from **56%** in 2007. [15]

Global Singlehood Trends:

- **Single-person households are prevalent in some countries:** In Sweden, **47%** of households consisted of one person in 2020, one of the highest rates globally. [16]
- **Single-person households are increasing globally:** The global percentage of single-person households rose from **23%** in 1985 to **28%** in 2018 and is projected to reach **35%** by 2050. [17]
- **Divorce rates are higher where gender equality is greater:** Divorce rates are higher in countries with greater gender equality, according to a 2016 study. [18]

The Social Lives of Singles: Debunking Myths

- **Active Social Lives:** Singles and those living alone are twice as likely as married individuals to go to bars, dance clubs, attend public events, and take art or music classes. [19]
- **Broad Social Networks:** Singles often have wider social networks and are more involved in their communities. [22]
- **Digital Age Influence:** Heavy Internet and social media users have larger and more diverse social networks, frequent public spaces, and are more likely to volunteer. [19]
- **Quality Over Quantity:** Research shows that the quality of social interactions, not their quantity, predicts loneliness. [22]

Later Life Singlehood

- **Well-Being Among Older Adults:** Older adults living alone in England report higher life satisfaction, more service provider contact, and similar cognitive and physical health compared to those living with others. [19]
- **Preference for Independence:** Older adults increasingly prefer living alone over institutional care or cohabiting with family. [19]

Author's Note of Caution

I want to be clear that the statistic (married couples with children have a lower divorce rate) does not mean children prevent divorce or make couples happier. Many couples stay together "for the children," sometimes modelling dysfunctional or unhealthy dynamics instead of separating. Often the fear is that separation may not be amicable or sustainable. This is a valid and real concern that each parent must weigh within their own personal circumstances.

If you have never faced this situation, it can feel easy to form an opinion. But unless you have lived it, you do not carry the consequences of that choice. We should neither applaud, judge, nor shame parents for choosing to stay married or to separate when children are involved. A healthy and safe home is always the ideal outcome. What matters most is recognising that it is not the presence of children that prevents divorce, but the ways in which the responsibility of raising dependent children shapes the choices couples make.

REFERENCES FOR THIS BOOK

Validated Global Statistics

[1] Pew Research Center. (2021). Rising Share of U.S. Adults Are Living Without a Spouse or Partner.

[2] Pew Research Center. (2021). The Changing Landscape of American Family Life.

[3] U.S. Census Bureau. (2021). Estimated Median Age at First Marriage: 1890 to Present.

[4] Stepler, R. (2017). Led by Baby Boomers, divorce rates climb for America's 50+ population. Pew Research Center.

[5] American Psychological Association. (2020). Marriage and Divorce.

[6-10] National Center for Health Statistics. (2019). First Marriages in the United States: Data From the 2011–2015 National Survey of Family Growth.

[11] Statista Research Department. (2024). Number of widowed people in Canada 2000-2022.

[12] U.S. Census Bureau. (2020). America's Families and Living Arrangements: 2020.

[13] eHarmony (2023). "Get Who Gets You Survey 2023." Retrieved from eHarmony.

[14] ListWithClever.com (2023). "Is Marriage Popularity Declining? Insights From a National Survey of Americans." Retrieved from ListWithClever.

[15] Pew Research Center. (2017). The share of Americans living without a partner has increased, especially among young adults.

[16] Statistics Sweden. (2021). Households in Sweden.

[17] United Nations. (2019). Household Size and Composition Around the World.

[18] Rosenfeld, M. J. (2016). How Couples Meet and Stay Together.

[19] Klinenberg, E. (2012). Going Solo: The Extraordinary Rise and Surprising Appeal of Living Alone.

[20] U.S. Census Bureau. (2021). Marital Status in the United States.

[21] Mbakile, S. (2021). Why Divorced Women in Their 40s-50s are Embracing Singlehood. Luvish.

[22] DePaulo, B. (2007). Singled Out: How Singles Are Stereotyped, Stigmatized, and Ignored, and Still Live Happily Ever After.

[23] Statistics Sweden. (2016). As cited in DiVA Portal, "The widowhood effect."

[24] The Loomba Foundation. (2015). World Widow Report: A Global Overview of Deprivation Faced by Widows.

[25] Vanier Institute. (2024). The percentage of older adults who are widowed has declined.

Selected Works Quoted and Researched

• Baumeister, Roy F., & Tierney, John. (2011). *Willpower: Rediscovering the Greatest Human Strength*. Penguin Press.

• Brown, Brené. (2015). *Rising Strong*. Spiegel & Grau.

• Covey, Stephen R. (1989). *The 7 Habits of Highly Effective People*. Free Press.

• DePaulo, Bella. (2006). *Singled Out: How Singles Are Stereotyped, Stigmatized, and Ignored, and Still Live Happily Ever After*. St. Martin's Press.

• Gray, Catherine. (2018). *The Unexpected Joy of Being Single*. Aster.

• Hale, Mandy. (2013). *The Single Woman: Life, Love, and a Dash of Sass*. Thomas Nelson.

• Hicks, Esther, & Hicks, Jerry. (2009). *The Vortex: Where the Law of Attraction Assembles All Cooperative Relationships*. Hay House.

- Jung, Carl Gustav. (1963). *Memories, Dreams, Reflections*. Pantheon. (Optional, if you keep the depression quote.)

- Kern Lima, Jamie. (2024). *Worthy: How to Believe You Are Enough and Transform Your Life*. Gallery Books.

- Klinenberg, Eric. (2012). *Going Solo: The Extraordinary Rise and Surprising Appeal of Living Alone*. Penguin Press.

- Kornfield, Jack. (1993). *A Path with Heart: A Guide Through the Perils and Promises of Spiritual Life*. Bantam.

- Kornfield, Jack. (2017). *No Time Like the Present: Finding Freedom, Love, and Joy Right Where You Are*. Atria Books.

- Nguyen, Joseph. (2022). *Don't Believe Everything You Think: Why Your Thinking Is the Beginning and End of Suffering*. Joseph Nguyen.

- Reber, Deborah. (2003). *Chicken Soup for the Teenage Soul: The Real Deal*. HCI.

- Rohn, Jim. (1991). *The Five Major Pieces to the Life Puzzle*. Jim Rohn International.

- Taleb, Nassim Nicholas. (2012). *Antifragile: Things That Gain from Disorder*. Random House.

- Tolle, Eckhart. (1997). *The Power of Now: A Guide to Spiritual Enlightenment*. New World Library.

- Kim, John. (2021). *Single on Purpose: Redefine Everything. Find Yourself First*. HarperOne.

ACKNOWLEDGMENTS

To my child, Koda

> You are my motivation and my reason for always wanting to grow, heal, and break cycles of ancestral pain. You inspire me to become the best version of myself, for you and for me.

To my mom and dad,

Thank you for making me feel loved and cared for in your own ways. From your strengths and your struggles, I learned lessons that shaped the woman I am today.

Mom, I honour your patience, generosity, and the sacrifices you made. Thank you for the deep conversations, the fun moments, and for wiping my tears after every heartbreak.

Dad, your kindness and encouragement gave me confidence, and I will always remember our trips to the markets, the game reserves, and the chats we shared in the backyard over a meal.

There are parts of my childhood I wish had been different, and life brought stresses none of us expected. Yet I know now that no journey is perfect. As a parent myself, I see more clearly that each generation carries both strengths and unhealed wounds, and that we are all doing our best with what we have. My hope is that future generations will inherit more healing, softer boundaries, and kinder childhoods. I treasure the laughter, the care, and the shared treats that lightened my childhood, and I hold close the love you gave and the foundation, though imperfect, that continues to help me grow.

To my friends,

To the handful of my closest friends who stood beside me during my divorce, thank you for holding space for both my fears, hopes and dreams.

To my readers,

Thank you for meeting these pages with your courage and honesty. It is no small thing to walk your own path. I am honoured to share this part of the journey with you.

To the authors, researchers, and thought leaders quoted throughout this book,

Thank you for your insights, clarity, and lived wisdom. Your words have not only shaped these pages, but have walked with me on the path toward deeper understanding. I'm grateful for the perspective you bring and the conversations your work continues to inspire.

To my cats,

To my three cats, Mune, Taiko and Whisp, thank you for being my quiet companions throughout this journey. A special thanks to Mune, who kept me company through countless writing hours when the task of finishing this book felt relentless and exhausting. Your warmth, purring and steady gaze reminded me why I was working so hard, to build a brighter future for us all.

In celebration and memory of:

This book would not be complete without acknowledging the loved ones who have passed, yet left their mark on my life in ways that continue to inspire me to be the best version of myself.

- Frans, your whistle, your quirky words, and your steady encouragement always meant more than I could say.
- Keith, you made me feel welcome and proud to see the world through a different lens. Your loyalty was consistent and always unwavering.
- Mona, the thought of you watching over me and my child has brought comfort and company across the years.

I am also grateful to my guides and protectors, seen and unseen, for the many ways they have helped me find strength, direction and peace.

My wish for you all,

May you always walk gently in your own truth, finding strength in quiet moments and courage in your becoming. May you embrace love without losing yourself and let go when it is time.

May you remember your worth, even on the days you doubt it, and let your life reflect the freedom of your deepest values. Wherever your path leads, may you move forward with kindness, clarity and the calm certainty that you are enough.

love Jace

ABOUT THE AUTHOR

Jace writes for people who are already paying attention to their inner lives, even when they are unsure what to do with what they notice.

Her work explores singlehood, separation, and emotional autonomy without urgency, instruction, or self improvement frameworks. She is interested in how people recognise misalignment, how they move through transitions quietly, and how steadiness can return without spectacle or performance.

Jace is the author of **Knowing When to Leave,** which sits with the threshold of separation, and Dare to be Single, which speaks to the rebuilding that follows. While the

 books are connected, they are written for different phases of the same journey.

She lives in Australia and believes that clarity often arrives slowly, that discomfort can carry information, and that people are allowed to choose peace without needing a dramatic reason.

> *There is a moment when you realise that no more conversation will fix it. No waiting for the right time. Once clarity arrives, it cannot be unseen."*
>
> — JACE STERLING, *KNOWING WHEN TO LEAVE*

www.ingramcontent.com/pod-product-compliance
Lightning Source LLC
Chambersburg PA
CBHW031100080526
44587CB00011B/764